The Sacred Heart of Jesus

THE SACRED HEART OF JESUS

MEDITATIONS AND PRAYERS

FR. BERNARD HÄRING, CSSR

Catholic. Pastoral. Trusted.

Imprimi Potest: Kevin Zubel, CSsR, Provincial
Denver Province, the Redemptorists

Published by Liguori Publications
Liguori, Missouri 63057

Liguori Publications, a nonprofit corporation,
is an apostolate of the Redemptorists (Redemptorists.com).

800-325-9521 Web: Liguori.org

*The Sacred Heart of Jesus:
Meditations and Prayers*
by Fr. Bernard Häring, CSsR

Copyright © 2025 Liguori Publications

ISBN 978-0-7648-2878-2
E-ISBN 978-0-7648-7261-7

Catalog in Publication data has been applied for with the
Library of Congress

All rights reserved. No part of this publication may be reproduced, stored in a retrieval system, or transmitted in any form or by any means—electronic, mechanical, photocopy, recording, or any other—except for brief quotations in printed reviews, without the prior written permission of Liguori Publications.

Scripture texts are taken from *The New English Bible*.
© The Delegates of the Oxford University Press and the Syndics of the Cambridge University Press 1961, 1970. Reprinted by permission.

Previously published in 1983 as *Heart of Jesus: Symbol of Redeeming Love,* Liguori Publications.

The Queen's Work
Liguori Publications has revived *The Queen's Work* imprint to support the needs of the people of God who desire a life of greater piety and devotion, and to encourage the positive spiritual energy that is present in the Church today.

Printed in the United States of America
25 26 27 28 29 / 5 4 3 2 1
First Edition

Cover Design: Wendy Barnes
Cover image: detail from a Holy card depicting the Sacred Heart of Jesus, c. 1880. Auguste Martin collection, University of Dayton Libraries / Wikimedia

CONTENTS

Introduction 9

1) God Loved Us First 19

2) God's Love Knows No Bounds 29

3) Love Cries Out for Love 39

4) God Loves the Sinner 49

5) Late Did I Come to Love You 57

6) Mary's Role in Her Son's Mission 65

7) God's Love in Revelation 73

8) Only Love Counts 81

9) Our Failure to Love 89

10) Heart of Jesus, Healer of Our Hearts 97

11) Only Love Can Atone 105

12) Atoning Value of Suffering 113

13) Personal Consecration to the Sacred Heart 121

14) World Consecration to the Sacred Heart 133

15) Family Consecration to the Sacred Heart 143

16) Streams of Living Water 151

17) Heart of Jesus and God's People 159

18) Eucharistic Heart of Jesus.. 167

19) Learning to Love in the Heart of Jesus 177

20) Union in the Heart of Jesus... 185

21) Heart of Jesus, the Good Shepherd.............................. 193

22) Heart of Jesus, the Divine Physician........................... 201

23) Jesus, Our Humble-Hearted Ideal................................ 211

24) Love Conquers All.. 219

25) Love Sets Us Free 227

26) Heart of Jesus and the Paschal Mystery 237

27) Heart of Jesus, Source of All Joy...................................245

28) Heart of Jesus, Human Symbol of Divine Love 253

29) Heart of Jesus, Victor Over Godlessness..................... 261

30) Heart of Jesus, Source of Peace in Our World...........267

"The symbol of the heart has often been used to express the love of Jesus Christ. Some have questioned whether this symbol is still meaningful today. Yet living as we do in an age of superficiality, rushing frenetically from one thing to another without really knowing why, and ending up as insatiable consumers and slaves to the mechanisms of a market unconcerned about the deeper meaning of our lives, all of us need to rediscover the importance of the heart."

> "Dilexit nos" of the Holy Father Francis
> on the human and divine love
> of the heart of Jesus Christ (2)

INTRODUCTION

All of humanity—every man and woman and child—needs redemption. This is especially true of the innermost self, the heart, which is often wounded, hurt, misguided, disturbed, cold, and unyielding. Our first parents' fall from grace did not render their hearts—and ours—incapable of action. Evil thoughts, desires, plans, and deeds may arise from the heart, but, from its deepest depths comes a longing, a cry for redemption, liberty, and true love, that makes its presence felt.

It is in the heart that redemption begins to function and to change the person and the world. Redemption and the healing of people and their relationships come from God, from his loving designs and "thoughts of peace." They become actual events whenever they touch the human heart with his love.

In the heart of Jesus, the Father's love meets us in incarnate reality and in the most tangible way. From that heart arises the perfect response of human love to the Father. Jesus, who comes from the "bosom of the Father," wants nothing less than to flood our hearts with his own overflowing love, thus making us participants in the love of the triune God, present and visible in his Sacred Heart.

The Church, through her devotion to the heart of Jesus, wants to waken us to this liberating truth to effect a most profound revolution: the conversion of the human heart, without which there is no effective redemption of the world.

Godlessness, in all its many forms is, above all, a perversion of the human heart. It indicates that we have lost our center; we have gone astray in our inmost being, in our hidden thoughts and desires.

"Heart" is a key concept of humanity. Scarcely any other word recurs so often in holy Scripture. The Bible speaks of the human heart in various ways: as the depth and center of our being, as conscience, as the inmost calling to love, as being created and recreated for redeemed love. But it also speaks of the heart of God, who reveals himself simply as Love—in loving deeds and words, in turning his countenance to us, and in drawing our hearts to himself.

Integrity of heart is the guarantee of healthy human relationships. The word "heart" is both a symbolic and a realistic expression for knowing lovingly. We express this in a very special way when we say "heart meets heart." In everyday language, in popular songs, and in great literature, attention centers on the heart when a person is deeply moved by the love shown by others or by the Other and, equally, if a great love meets rejection or is otherwise distressed.

In the devotion to the Sacred Heart of Jesus, as it has evolved throughout the centuries and as proposed by the teaching and liturgy of the Church, there is conscious concentration on both the symbolic and palpable reality of the heart, particularly in the personal encounter of our hearts with the heart of Jesus.

In this light, we come to see and to contemplate the whole of revelation as the dynamic, attractive communication of divine love in and through a human heart that is at the same time divine. And we also see that the noblest vocation of all men and women is to be called to love.

The devotion to the Sacred Heart of our Redeemer is a privileged pathway to true religion: "the cult of love" and "synthesis of the mystery of our religion," as Pope Pius XII expressed it. Its purpose is the triumph also of God's own love—through his grace in the hearts of the redeemed—over the assaults of hatred, enmity, hardness of heart, terrorism, and war. Above all, it is a matter of God's merciful love transforming us in our inmost selves, enabling us to form loving relationships and to be "light for the world."

True veneration of the Sacred Heart of Jesus is more than just a private devotion tending toward excessive sentimentality. In the heart of Jesus, Word Incarnate, the love and mercy of the triune God for the salvation of all humanity are revealed. The divine purpose is nothing less than to bring humankind back to the love of God, from which it has gone astray.

The heart of Jesus tells us how great God's love for humankind is. The heart of Jesus also demonstrates how devastating it is for our innermost selves and for all the world if this love is refused. This redemptive love wants to touch and transform us to make us light for the world—a new people with healthy relationships.

Inseparable from the Sacred Heart devotion is a deeply felt pain for having offended the all-holy and all-loving God. We all know how much this dimension of repentance needs attention today. Those who are seized by the love of Jesus' heart grieve over the sins of humanity, and they long for reparation.

This devotion, which for centuries has been a great blessing, has diminished during the last decades, at least in some countries. The causes are manifold: disinterest in traditional devotions, lack of enthusiasm for spiritual realities, enslavement to consumerism, a seemingly constant barrage of sound and distraction, and minds numbed by social media. Frequently, too, there is ignorance or error about the theological foundations of the devotion itself.

Our points of reference here are holy Scripture, the liturgy, and the directions given by the successors of Peter, especially the encyclical *Haurietis Aquas*, written by Pius XII in 1956, which integrates the main lines of thought of his predecessors. Also included is the rich harvest of tradition dating back to the time of the Fathers of the Church. Important as the influence of St. Margaret Mary Alacoque (1647–1690) has been for the devotion to the Sacred Heart, it would be a grave error to think that the devotion started with this seventeenth-century saint.

With great fervor, the ancient Fathers of the Church meditated and reflected on the wounded heart of Jesus. His heart, which opened for us, even after his death, the "port of salvation" became for us the "refuge of sinners" from which spring the Church and all her sacraments: the streams of grace. With holy envy, they recalled the beloved disciple, the evangelist of love, who at the Last Supper was nearest to the heart of Jesus. Within this context, they brought together the many texts of the Old and New Testaments, which tell of the heart-love of God and the image of God as the Father of Israel, the Divine Physician, the Good Shepherd, the Divine Spouse who, despite all the sins of humankind, remains faithful to his first love, his people.

Saint Anselm of Canterbury (1093–1109) did much to revitalize this great heritage in his time. Saint Bernard of Clairvaux (1090–1153) was an abiding influence by his deep devotion to the humanity of Jesus and his great love of the Crucified who yearned to draw us all to his heart and thus to the Father. He sees in the heart of Jesus, opened for us, the revelation of the deepest secrets of God, the "thoughts of his heart."

Not less was the impact of St. Francis of Assisi (1181–1226) and his Order. We look to Francis as the disciple of Jesus, glowing with love, so near to the heart of Jesus that he shared with the Beloved Master the wound of his heart and the wounds of his hands and feet. And St. Bonaventure (1221–1274) was a great exponent of this devotion.

The devotion to the Sacred Heart was at its best during the thirteenth century, especially in the monastery of the Benedictine nuns in Helfta, Germany under St. Mechtilde of Hackeborn (1240–1298) and St. Gertrude the Great (1256–1302). Here, the contemplation of Jesus' heart, overflowing with love and drawing all sensitive hearts to himself, was not just an occasional devotion but was the focal point of piety. This devotion drew the hearts of many people to a tender love of Jesus.

The Dominican Order, too, can claim a good number of fervent promoters of this devotion, beginning with St. Dominic (1170–1221), the founder, and its greatest theologians, from St. Albert the Great (1206–1280) and St. Thomas Aquinas (1225–1274) to the mystical school of Meister Eckhart (1260–1328) and Johannes Tauler (1300–1361).

The role of Blessed Henry Suso (1295–1366) was unique. His love of Jesus' heart, pierced for us all, knew no bounds. As a charismatic poet and preacher, he inspired great numbers to practice this veneration of the Sacred Heart. In his deep devotion, he saw Jesus in his full humanity and strength, the One who made himself humble to heal our tendency to pride.

In his prayers, Henry frequently spoke to "Divine Wisdom," most loving and most worthy of love. He was overwhelmed by her love for us. He exulted when she said to him, "Be wise, my son…bring joy to my heart" (Proverbs 27:11). Enraptured, he responded, "I embrace you with my heart's burning longing." His spirituality was one of constant praise of God's mercy, particularly as revealed in Jesus' suffering heart. The desired fruit of this loving praise is a gift of such serenity and peace that the disciple of Jesus can feel for suffering people the deepest compassion and a generous love that offers the needed sacrifices.

Henry Suso hears Divine Wisdom telling him, "In the great bitterness of my suffering, my boundless love itself is like the sun showing itself in its splendor, like the beauty of the rose in its fragrance, like a mighty fire in its heat. Listen with devotion, therefore, to how much has been suffered for you!" At another time, Divine Wisdom instructs him, "Through the open wound, enter into my heart wounded for love, and lovingly abide and rest in it." Poet and priest, he prays and sings, "Open, O Lord, the shrine of your love; open to me, O Jesus mine, thine heart. Keep free my heart from false love and all its glitter."

Suso also tells us how he gained from Divine Wisdom a new understanding of expiation. When he tortured his body in his longing to share in Jesus' loving suffering, Divine Wisdom gently told him to stop such nonsense and instead to abandon himself to the Father's will. In response, he calmly accepted all the suffering that the sharing of his love with all people brings with it or requires for the sake of its purity. Once, when he was shamefully defamed, his reaction was, "I shall bring this grievance before Jesus' heart, grieved by love for us." He was grateful that, in the school of suffering, Divine Wisdom prepared him for serene and peaceful conformity with her will. The strength of his love for the loving heart of Jesus was for him also the source of a generous and patient zeal for the salvation of all.

Eckhart's, Tauler's, and especially Henry Suso's writings had a long-lasting influence in France and Italy, as well as in Germany. In Italy, both the Dominicans and the Franciscans promoted the devotion to the Sacred Heart of Jesus and reached many laypeople, especially through the influence of St. Catherine of Siena (1347–1380). In France, the influence of these people was deep and lasting, especially through translations of Suso's works.

A happy development came about through a combination of the mystical approach and the sacramental vision. It reached a high peak in St. John Eudes (1601–1680), the pioneer of the liturgy of the Sacred Heart of Jesus. He authored liturgical texts for the celebration of the Eucharist and for the breviary in honor of the Sacred Heart; these texts were allowed in France by the local ecclesiastical authorities beginning in 1668.

INTRODUCTION

The spirituality and zeal of St. Margaret Mary Alacoque for the liturgy of the Sacred Heart follows the same direction as that of St. John Eudes. It is not at all a new beginning, as some opponents of this form of devotion thought, but only a new emphasis within a rich tradition, with particular interest in its liturgical expression. Its urgent appeal for expiation and conversion to merciful love is its main characteristic.

Some formulations by the saint, and especially by those who spread her message, met considerable opposition and a spell of aloofness by the Holy See. But the authority of St. Alphonsus Liguori (1696–1787), who himself fervently venerated the Sacred Heart, settled the problem. It seems that some were holding that the heart is the seat of all affection. But St. Alphonsus maintained that such an assertion is contrary to the insights of science and is in no way necessary for the purpose and meaning of this devotion. In the extensive introduction to his treatise *Novena to the Sacred Heart*, he insisted on the basic symbolism of the broader concept of heart in the Bible and tradition.

On this basis, St. Alphonsus gave strong support to the petition of the Polish bishops who, with the Archconfraternity of the Sacred Heart in Rome, had asked for approbation of the public liturgy, which was granted by Pope Clement XIII in 1765.

In 1856, Pope Pius IX made the liturgical celebration of the feast of the Sacred Heart of Jesus obligatory in the whole Church. Pope Leo XIII deepened the understanding of the consecration to the Sacred Heart of Jesus and showed the relationship between the veneration of the Sacred Heart and the salvation of the world.

The doctrinal development of the devotion to the Sacred Heart is excellently summarized in the encyclical *Haurietis Aquas* of Pope Pius XII. By no means does he disavow the disclosures that came from the humble Visitation nun, St. Margaret Mary Alacoque; rather, he explicitly insists that the veneration of the Sacred Heart of Jesus is not based on private revelations but on the Bible and tradition.

1

GOD LOVED US FIRST

Everyone who loves is a child of God and knows God, but the unloving know nothing of God. For God is love, and his love was disclosed to us in this: that he sent his only Son into the world to bring us life. The love I speak of is not our love for God, but the love he showed to us in sending his Son as the remedy for the defilement of our sins. If God thus loved us, dear friends, we in turn are bound to love one another.

1 JOHN 4:8–11

Meditation on this First Letter of John should serve as the best introduction to the basic meaning of the veneration of the Sacred Heart of Jesus. The very first words of the letter indicate one of the primary concerns of this great witness to divine and human love. John shares with his readers the most intimate and encompassing experience of love and of the nearness of God in Christ Jesus. "It was there from the beginning; we have heard it; we have seen it with our own eyes; we looked upon it and felt it with our own hands; and it is of this we tell. Our theme is the word of life.…What we have seen and heard we declare to you, so that you and we together may share in a common life, that life which we share with the Father and his Son Jesus Christ" (1 John 1:1–3).

In this text, the heart of John, who has felt the very beating of the loving heart of Jesus, speaks to us. He testifies that God's own love has made itself visible in the Word Incarnate. It is a tangible love that wants to touch us bodily and in that inmost self whose symbol is the heart. "This is how we may recognize the Spirit of God: every spirit which acknowledges that Jesus Christ has come in the flesh is from God, and every spirit which does not thus acknowledge Jesus is not from God" (1 John 4:2–3).

The heart of Jesus, whose pulsation was felt first by his Blessed Mother when she bore him in her womb and that lived and suffered for all of us. The heart whose anguished concern for us bathed Jesus' body in a bloody sweat and was pierced by the soldier's lance even after he had died for us. This heart best symbolizes and incorporates the central truth of our faith in the Incarnation of the Son of God.

In this most sensitive human heart, the love of the Father and for the Father burned and spread its light and warmth. This heart loved the Father perfectly in the name of all creation. And it is in this heart that we see the love by which the Father has loved us.

With Johannine affection, St. John Henry Newman addresses Jesus: "My God, my Savior, I adore thy Sacred Heart, for that heart is the seat and source of all thy tenderest human affections for us sinners. It is the instrument and organ of thy love. It did beat for us. It yearned for us. It ached for us and for our salvation. It was on fire through zeal that the glory of God might be manifested in and by us. It is the channel through which has come to us all thine overflowing human affection, all thy divine charity towards us. All thine incomprehensible compassion for us, as God and Man, as our Creator and Redeemer and Judge, has come to us, and comes in one inseparable mingled stream, through that Sacred Heart. O most sacred Symbol and Sacrament of Love, divine and human, in its fullness thou didst save me by thy divine strength and thy human affection, and then at length by that wonderworking blood, wherewith thou didst overflow."

In the heart of Jesus, most loving and willing to suffer for love's sake, creation and the history of salvation find their center and summit. As we gratefully contemplate this heart, we understand in a new way that God created the world and humankind for no less a purpose than to have sharers of his own blissful love.

In the heart of the Son of God, there is the unsurpassable reality of sharing in the Father's love and in the power of the Spirit of truth and love. Here, in this perfect spectrum and symbol, divine and human love are brought together. The Father's love flows to his Son and, in him and through him, to humankind; the purest human love, the authentic love of humankind, flows to the Father from the heart of the Son.

For God, who is love in triune fullness, there would be no motive for the creation of humankind other than his overflowing love and his total freedom to share his love and to call us to this sharing. He wants us, his people, to be not only recipients of his love but also concelebrants—joyous sharers of the very love with which the Father loves the Son and the Son responds to the Father in the mutuality of the Spirit. This pertains to the most profound meaning of God's creation of man and woman in his own image and likeness.

The more we respond to God's love and his call to return his love, and the more we come to understand what it means to love and be loved by Jesus and with Jesus, the more we become an image of God in reality and truth. Here on earth, we are students in the best sense when we learn, in and from the heart of Jesus, to adore the Father and to share in his and Jesus' love for all people. Our final goal is the eternal feast of love with God in the communion of saints.

Sinful humanity imprisons itself in its own perverted self-love, in the loveless fortress of self-defense. All sins are marked by lovelessness, by a decreasing capacity to discern what true love is and a reluctance to strive for love at all. Utter lovelessness is godlessness, having no share in God who is Love. What some scientists predict about a final dissolution of the world through a kind of loss of energy is only a pale image of a world frozen in lovelessness.

Praise be to God that in his great love, he remains faithful to his design! Despite the sinfulness of humankind, he follows "his heart's desire" (Jeremiah 30:24). Only a heart of stone will not be moved by hearing God's word: "I will heal their apostasy; of my own bounty will I love them" (Hosea 14:4).

Faithful to the thoughts of his heart, God sent his beloved Son to redeem rebellious humanity and to fulfill this mission by the power of his merciful love. As believers, our response can be only amazement, praise, and boundless gratitude. Our wonder will never cease when we meditate on these words: "So the Word became flesh; he came to dwell among us, and we saw his glory, such glory as befits the Father's only Son, full of grace and truth....No one has ever seen God; but God's own Son, he who is nearest to the Father's heart, he has made him known" (John 1:14–18).

The fact that he "who is nearest to the Father's heart"

has come in the flesh to make known the love of the Father prompted the Church in apostolic times to venerate the heart of Jesus, whose love comes from the Father and leads to the Father.

It is not enough to see Jesus as the model, prototype, and object of our love. There is more. He has come to share with us his own love for the Father and the Father's love for us. He unites our hearts with his own when we open ourselves to him in faith and trust. By his Spirit, Christ enables us to grasp "God's secret. That secret is Christ himself; in him lie hidden all God's treasures of wisdom and knowledge" (Colossians 2:2–3).

Paul's teaching is that we believers have "life in Christ Jesus." Hence his urgent appeal: "Live your lives in union with him. Be rooted in him; be built in him; be consolidated in the faith you were taught; let your hearts overflow with thankfulness" (Colossians 2:6–7).

A heart touched by the heart of Jesus is, indeed, "overflowing with thankfulness." This is the constant, joyful acknowledgment that God has first loved us and that the love he has manifested to us in Jesus is utterly undeserved and cannot dwell in ungrateful hearts. One of Christianity's oldest songs of praise, which comes to us in the introduction of Paul's Letter to the Ephesians, expresses thankfulness for the amazing graciousness of God's revelation in Jesus: "Praise be to the God and Father of our Lord Jesus Christ, who has bestowed on us in Christ every spiritual blessing in the heavenly realms. In Christ, he chose us before the world was founded, to be dedicated, to be without blemish in his sight, to be full of love; and he destined us—such was his will and pleasure—to be accepted as his sons through Jesus Christ, in order that the glory of his gracious gift, so graciously bestowed on us in his Beloved, might redound to his praise" (Ephesians 1:3–6).

For the Apostle to the Gentiles, ingratitude, insensitivity, and hardness of heart are marks of "misguided minds...plunged in darkness" and of a perverted culture. (See Romans 1:21–28.)

In Jesus' warnings about the eschatological birth pangs, he points to the greatest evil: "As lawlessness spreads, men's love for one another will grow cold" (Matthew 24:12). In the New Testament, "lawlessness" is, above all, lack of love, the total refusal of the liberating law of love that Jesus has granted us.

In a decisive religious experience, St. Margaret Mary Alacoque saw Jesus painfully shaken by the coldness of so many hearts. So few people were moved to honor his heart in fervent love and in compensation for the wounds inflicted by this thanklessness. When the saint complained to the Lord about her own incapacity, such a flame of love came from the heart of the glorified Lord that she was afraid of being burned by its fire. But Jesus told her, "I shall be your strength."

The meaning of this symbolic experience is central to

the devotion to the Sacred Heart. It solicits abiding gratitude for God's initiative in revealing his love to us through Jesus' heart pierced for us and his blood shed for us; faith-filled trust that the heart of the risen Christ will never stop beating with love for us; a great longing to see Jesus praised by all.

We yearn to see our love purified and strengthened, united with the love of Jesus and of all his true disciples, so that his love will be felt by ever more people. And we want our hearts to be so filled by Jesus' own love that, through us, the love of God and of Jesus may reach many hearts.

In the liturgy in honor of the Sacred Heart, renewed in 1928, there resounds Jesus' urgent invitation: "If anyone is thirsty, let him come to me; whoever believes in me, let him drink" (John 7:37). Those who truly venerate the Sacred Heart not only long to refresh themselves at the fountain of salvation but also thirst, above all, to see God loved and honored by everyone. For devoted disciples of Christ, the danger of a deadly coldness in so many hearts is frightening. They are willing to do everything in their power to draw others to the same love of the heart of Jesus so that these people, too, may be transformed by it.

Our technically developed world is in great danger of losing life's center—the inner resources of people's hearts—and thus losing the wholeness of vision. In this threatening situation, we must not fail to promote the veneration of the Sacred Heart. In his encyclical *Miserentissimus Redemptor*, Pope Leo XIII wrote these words of lasting relevance: "In the Sacred Heart of Jesus, there is given to us a symbol of the unchangeable love of Christ which, by itself, moves us to the response of love."

Prayer

Opening Prayer of the Votive Mass of the Sacred Heart

Clothe us, Lord God, with the virtues of the Heart of your Son and set us aflame with his love, that, conformed to his image, we may merit a share in eternal redemption. Through our Lord Jesus Christ, your Son, who lives and reigns with you in the unity of the Holy Spirit, one God, for ever and ever.

Amen.

2

GOD'S LOVE KNOWS NO BOUNDS

It was before the Passover festival. Jesus knew that his hour had come and that he must leave this world and go to the Father. He had always loved his own who were in the world, and now he was to show the full extent of his love.

JOHN 13:1

There must be no limit to your goodness, as your heavenly Father's goodness knows no bounds.

MATTHEW 5:48

GOD'S LOVE KNOWS NO BOUNDS

This is the central truth of revelation: "God is Love." These words concern not only the innermost life of the triune God but also contain the good news about God's relationship with the created world and especially with humankind.

Indeed, God has gone to the utmost limits to make his infinite love known to us in a way that touches our hearts, minds, and wills. He speaks the language of the heart, flowing from the heart of Jesus pierced for us, and he sends us his Holy Spirit so that our hearts can become sensitive, affectionate, and grateful for this sublime love.

God speaks to us through all of creation. Its beauty and bounty are an assurance of God's overflowing, attractive love. Heaven and earth sing the praise of the Creator, who reveals his perfection and majesty in all his works. Creation belongs to the essence of beauty that it speaks to the whole person, inviting admiration, reverence, and praise. A heart sensitive to beauty cannot but wonder: if the beauty of the created reality fills our hearts and minds with delight, how much more glorious must be the beauty of the Creator!

A person's countenance becomes particularly beautiful when he or she receives love and responds to it. Our hearts, then, rejoice, knowing that this is a wonderful reflection of God's own countenance turning to us in boundless love. The hearts of parents beat with joy on seeing the smile of their beloved child—which in itself is an amazing response to the love the child has received from them. It is foolish to ignore the fact that all this flows from God, our Creator, and invites our response to his gracious love.

Yet, this is only a prelude to the supreme revelation of God's love in the Incarnation, life, death, and resurrection of his only Son. Creation of the world by the eternal Word was the first fascinating message from the Father. His Word thus eternally proclaims all his being and all his love. But even more wonderful is the fact that the Father sends us this Word in the flesh of the world, our own humanity. He comes to be for us "Emmanuel—God-with-us," "Son of Man," "One-of-us." The Word Incarnate, the "One-of-us," is the supreme investment not only of God's might but also, above all, of his eternal love in the created world.

God, our Creator, is also the supreme artist, making us into his own image, awakening us to the revelation of his love, and gracing us with the will to respond to it with all our being: our hearts, memories, minds, and wills. In the Word Incarnate, God has also become our brother, one of us, our dearest friend, our Savior, our Divine Physician. Holy Scripture uses an even more intimate image: God, the "spouse" of his people, and Jesus, the "spouse" of his Church and, indeed, of all redeemed humankind.

God speaks his love to us, addresses our heart and mind through his own substantial Word, who eternally breathes the Spirit of Love. But there is more! In his Incarnate Word, God enters into our deepest human misery—with the exception of sin—and he even takes upon himself the burden of our sin-solidarity. As "One-of-us," he becomes one with the poor, the oppressed, and the outcast so that he may bestow upon us the riches and honor of redeemed love. No earthly wealth or comfort should let us forget that he is the revelation of divine love and the one who, in the name of all the universe, gives to the Father the full response of boundless love, drawing us to his heart so that we may join him in this response.

The divine "One-of-us" who is "God-with-us" takes our suffering so much to heart that, shouldering our anguish and estrangement, he sheds his blood on the cross. Fully aware of his divine origin and his returning into his own in the glory of the Father, Jesus gives his unsurpassable, self-giving assent to atoning love. Facing the naked unbelief and hatred embodied in the dominating ruling religious class, he reveals the full extent of God's boundless love.

Surely, God did not set in motion the murderous assault on his beloved Servant and Son, Jesus. But in full knowledge of the abyss of human sinfulness, Father and Son, in the loving power of the Spirit, took this unique risk. Jesus came as leader of salvation-solidarity for all people. If sinful leaders and seducers of the people would go so far as to condemn the Son of Man, the "One-of-us," he would not shy away from this hideous pit of sin-solidarity. He extended himself to the limit to drink the bitter chalice of suffering.

Full of wonder at this unsurpassable ardor of God's love, Paul writes: "He did not spare his own Son, but gave him up for us all; and with this gift how can he fail to lavish upon us all he has to give?" (Romans 8:32). By "all he has to give," Paul means the absolute assurance of the victory of God's love. He had experienced it in his own conversion and election. "Then what can separate us from the love of Christ?…I am convinced that there is nothing in death or life, in the realm of the spirits or superhuman powers, in the world as it is or the world as it shall be, in the forces of the universe, in heights or depths—nothing in all Creation that can separate us from the love of God in Christ Jesus our Lord" (Romans 8:35–39).

Saint Alphonsus, like many other theologians, was faced time and again with the question of whether the only way the Son of God could atone for our sins was by suffering a terrible death on the cross. His firm answer was that death was not necessary, even in view of the horrible history of human sinfulness. Anything that the Incarnate Word did on earth would have been sufficient for atonement, because it was done with infinite love. For St. Alphonsus and other doctors of the Church, the decisive reason why the Word suffered death was because the Father desired to reveal no limit to the manifestation of his love.

In a profound, heartfelt manner, we all should realize that the goodness and nearness of God knows no bounds. Divine and redeeming love is victorious over the very depth of human deprivation. This is the power of the love that inflamed the Sacred Heart of Jesus. Through it, God wanted to speak to our hearts: "What more could I, in my great love, do for you?"

The beloved disciple—the one who was nearest to the heart of Jesus at the Last Supper—introduced the farewell discourses and the high-priestly prayer spoken there, with these words: "And now he was to show the full extent of his love" or, as some translate, "He loved them utterly to the end" (John 13:1). This refers to the bitter suffering and death that Jesus foresaw and that he accepted as the Father's will.

The Eucharist that Jesus instituted on that occasion was given as a testament to his disciples, as an abiding memorial for grateful memories. Jesus' utter self-giving—he "made himself nothing, assuming the nature of a slave" (Philippians 2:7)—in his Incarnation, life, suffering, and death thus continues in another mysterious way in the Eucharist. This is an essential feature in the self-revelation of the Word of God. So much has Jesus bound himself to us weak human beings in his Incarnation and suffering that, even after his death and resurrection, he wants to give us the most explicit sign of remaining "One-of-us," a total gift to us of his abiding presence.

The institution of the Eucharist at the Last Supper coincides with the solemn promise to send us the Holy Spirit. In the power of the Spirit, Jesus has given himself up for us. In the same power, he makes a gift of himself to us in the Eucharist and enables us, through the Spirit, to surrender ourselves to him. In granting this wonderful memorial, he wants to change our forgetfulness into a grateful, loving memory.

In all this, Jesus speaks to our hearts, especially if we contemplate it with our eyes and our minds fixed on his own Sacred Heart, pierced for us, opened to shower streams of grace upon us. In the presence of the risen Lord in the Eucharist, we know that his heart will never stop beating for us.

Prayer

Saint Alphonsus' *Novena to the Sacred Heart*

O heart of Jesus, most worthy of adoration, glowing with love for us who are created for this very love, how is it possible that you find so poor a response from people, even to the point of disregard? I, too, belonged to the ungrateful ones and did not know how to love you. Forgive me, my Jesus, this great sin of having refused my love to you who, by your own love, urged me to respond with a grateful heart. By withholding my love, I deserve the terrible punishment of being unable to love you. My beloved Redeemer, spare me this punishment. Compared with it, any other punishment would be small. Grant me the grace to love you; then I shall have no fear. Yet how could I fear such a terrible affliction, since I know that you command me to love you with all my heart?

Yes, my God, you want to be loved by me, and I want

nothing more than to love you who have loved me so much. O heart of my Jesus, you are my love. O, heart glowing with love, inflame my heart with love for you.

Keep me in your love forever so that there may never come a moment when I live without loving you. Let me rather die than show the world such ingratitude as to again disown your holy love. Never, O Jesus, never let this happen! I put my trust in your precious blood, which was shed for me, and I hope that I shall love you and that you love me forever. May this love between us last forever!

Mary, Mother of our beautiful Love, you yearn to see your Son loved; bind me so firmly to him with the bond of love that I cannot ever again be separated from him.

Amen.

3

LOVE CRIES OUT FOR LOVE

I have come to set fire to the earth, and how I wish it were already kindled! I have a baptism to undergo, and what constraint I am under until the ordeal is over!

LUKE 12:49

Jesus knows all too well the tremendous obstacles opposing his mission to set humanity free for redeemed and redeeming love. He has come from the Father to kindle the fire of true love. His heart is aflame with the desire to see the Father loved by all people. His yearning to inflame us by the fire of his own love is greater than the constraint with which he awaits the coming ordeal of death on the cross.

The heart of Jesus, pierced by our lovelessness yet opened as the fountain of love for us, perfectly symbolizes the truth that he, who is Love, cries out for love. The all-loving God wants to be loved by us. It belongs to the essence and dynamics of every true human love that it longs for love in response. Those who are not interested in this response can hardly claim that they really do love. Jesus solicits our love; we may even say he "courts" it by the efficacious means of communicating his own love to us. He knows that we cannot enter into the eternal feast of the triune love unless we learn here on earth to love our Creator and Redeemer. The blood baptism that he foresees and accepts is, indeed, anguishing, but because it is destined to become the sign of our blood kinship with him, he awaits the decisive hour when it will be consummated on the cross.

Jesus prays, "What am I to say? 'Father, save me from this hour. No, it was for this that I came to this hour. Father, glorify thy name.' A voice sounded from heaven: 'I have glorified it, and I will glorify it again'" (John 12:27–28).

The privileged hour in which the name of the Father is glorified embraces the three terrible hours of Jesus' agony on the cross. By his great love and trust, Jesus glorifies the name of the Father, and the Father glorifies his Son by this victory of love.

Jesus explains to his disciples an essential aspect of this glorification of the Father's name: "I shall draw all men to myself when I am lifted up from the earth." One might think that this "lifting up" refers exclusively to Christ's resurrection, but the evangelist makes clear what Jesus meant: "This he said to indicate the kind of death he was to die" (John 12:32–33).

O holy cross, sign of torture, now you have become the sign of redeeming love! The voice of the Father tells us what you mean for him and for us. You recall to our hearts through all the ages how much the heart of Jesus thirsts for our love, so that the name of the Father of all will be glorified.

Jesus' being lifted up on the cross is the first act of an ongoing drama. Lifted up to heavenly glory, Jesus sends us the Holy Spirit to draw us to his heart, which forever glorifies the Father, while manifesting his love for us and calling for love in return. He tells us that the Father, too, desires our love in loving knowledge of his name. "No man can come to me unless he is drawn by the Father who sent me" (John 6:44). The call for our love in return, united with Jesus' love, is the work of the whole Trinity.

Already in the Old Testament, God speaks the language of love calling for love in return: "It was I who taught Ephraim to walk, I who had taken them in my arms; but they did not know that I harnessed them in leading-strings and led them with bonds of love—that I had lifted them like a little child to my cheek, that I had bent down to feed them" (Hosea 11:3–4). Like many other texts, this reminds us that the most tender love of the human heart is a God-given experience that should lead us to an ever-deeper understanding of God's own love, the source of all human affections.

In the Book of Proverbs, we read, "My son, if you are wise at heart, my heart in its turn will be glad" (23:15). God wants us whole and wholly. His love wants to touch us, to move us in our deepest depths, to take hold of us and set us free for the full sharing of his own blissful love. We have to make the decision, and by opening ourselves to his love and grace, we are able to do so. "No servant can be slave of two masters" (Matthew 6:24).

If we make up our minds to seek first and above all else the kingdom of God and its saving justice (See Matthew 6:33), then we begin to savor the words of Jesus: "Where your treasure is, there will your heart be also" (Matthew 6:21). God will give us a new understanding of his love, an ever-increasing joy of being seized by his love and being called to intimate union with him. When we strive for nothing less than to love God with all our hearts, then we truly become "adorers of God in spirit and truth."

In Jesus, God shows himself thirsting for our love response. He himself is overflowing Love and the Center of all Creation. Only in this full response of love can we ourselves find the sense and purpose of our life, our completion, and our abiding joy.

God cannot accept a superficial, divided love as worthy of his majesty. Of this truth we are constantly reminded: "Hear, O Israel, the Lord is our God, one Lord, and you must love the Lord your God with all your heart and soul and strength. These commandments…are to be kept in your heart" (Deuteronomy 6:4–6).

If all the commandments and this gracious commandment are kept in our hearts, then we understand it as an appeal coming from the pierced heart of Jesus, and we can only wonder how anyone could ever refuse response to such an amazing love. How can we, who have been redeemed, ever cease rejoicing in this invitation to love our Savior? Captured by the love of Jesus and by his zeal for the glory of the Father, his disciples will yearn with him to see the Father loved by all. And this will be an added incentive to show greater zeal for the love of neighbor whom the Father has created.

The thought that so many saints in heaven and on earth have dedicated themselves to respond to God's love in union with the Sacred Heart of Jesus is an invitation to joy and praise. "Zion, cry out for joy; raise the shout of triumph, Israel....The Lord your God is in your midst...he will rejoice over you...he will show you his love once more" (Zephaniah 3:14, 17).

This rejoicing of God, while renewing our hearts with his love, must not be misunderstood as his needing our love response for his own fullness of beatitude. He does not love us out of a need for bliss but out of the superabundance of his own love and because of his design to make us sharers of his eternal feast of love. His joy in our response is simply a part of that love. The Sacred Heart of Jesus is the abiding symbol of this truth.

The insight that the all-holy God does not need our love has led some theologians to draw the false conclusion that God is not interested in being loved by us. What he wants, they say, is that we turn our love to our neighbor and thus render thanks for God's love. Such a theory contradicts the central truths of revelation and of basic human experience. No loving parent would say to his or her children, "I am not interested in your responding to my love for you; my only desire is that you love others." Such thinking would also undermine love of neighbor. How can a person whose parents have no interest in his or her love response be a loving brother or sister?

As Jesus draws us to his heart, the Father draws us to Jesus and himself. While doing so, God offers us a new heart, enabling us to join him in his feast of love and his love for all humankind.

The tradition of the devotion to the Sacred Heart expresses this truth in various images. Saint Albert the Great, as well as St. Gertrude the Great and St. Mechtilde, speak of an "exchange of hearts." We renounce our selfish love so that we may be fully inserted into his holy love. Thus, Jesus can dwell in our hearts, and we are at home in his loving heart. For that we pray: "Jesus, conform my heart with yours!"

This is also clearly expressed in the Johannine and Pauline theology of "life in Christ Jesus." Filled with love of Christ, the Apostle to the Gentiles can exult: "The life I now live is not my life, but the life which Christ lives in me" (Galatians 2:20).

We venerate St. Francis of Assisi, who was so thoroughly enamored of Jesus Crucified that he was found worthy by Jesus to be impressed with the wound of Jesus' pierced heart. The life of Francis, and of many other saints, tells us one thing: Love cries out for love! God the Father, who has called us through the love of Jesus, is truly interested in our response of love. Nothing is more urgent than loving God "with all our heart." This is the definite message from the saints, who also tell us that with God's grace, this is possible.

If we live consciously and gratefully according to the grace and message of baptism, confirmation, and the Eucharist, we shall realize ever more that we, too, are marked by the heart of Jesus. That heart, pierced for us and sealed by his precious blood, invites us—through the gift of the Spirit—to return love for love.

Prayer

Saint Alphonsus' *Novena to the Sacred Heart*

My dear Savior, I say with St. Augustine: You command me to love you and threaten me with punishment if I do not love you. But what more horrifying punishment, what more terrible disgrace can there be than to be deprived of your love? If, then, you wish to terrify me, threaten only that I would have to live without loving you, and this will frighten me more than the threat of hell. If, in the midst of hell's flames, the condemned could be inflamed by your love, hell would become paradise. And if, on the other hand, the blessed in heaven were unable to love you, paradise would become hell.

O my beloved Lord, I realize that by my sins I have deserved to be deprived of your grace and condemned not to love you, but I know that you still tell me to love you, and I feel a great desire to do so. This desire is your own gracious gift. Give me, then, the strength and also the fidelity to put this into practice. Help me, so that now and forever I can truthfully and with all my heart repeat, "My God, I love you. You desire my love and I desire yours."

Forget then, O Jesus, the displeasure I have caused you in the past. Love cries out for love. I shall not abandon you; you will never abandon me. Forever you will love me, and forever I shall love you. My dear Savior, I put my trust in your merits. Permit me, a sinner who has so gravely offended you, to love you.

Immaculate Virgin Mary, assist me; pray to Jesus for me.

Amen.

GOD LOVES THE SINNER

For at the very time when we were still powerless, then Christ died for the wicked. Even for a just man, one of us would hardly die, though perhaps for a good man one might actually brave death; but Christ died for us while we were yet sinners, and that is God's own proof of his love toward us. And so, since we have now been justified by Christ's sacrificial death, we shall all the more certainly be saved through him from final retribution. For if, when we were God's enemies, we were reconciled to him through the death of his Son, how much more, now that we are reconciled, shall we be saved by his life! But that is not all: we also exult in God through our Lord Jesus, through whom we have now been granted reconciliation.

ROMANS 5:6–11

GOD LOVES THE SINNER

In the course of a cruel battle in Russia during World War II, when many medical orderlies had been lost, I heard calls for help from a neighboring unit. Despite extreme exhaustion, I ran to look for the wounded man. He was in a hopeless condition. After applying first aid, I told him, "I am a priest," and I asked if he would like to receive the sacraments, including holy Communion. When he heard this, there was a sudden change. Astonished and with great joy, he said over and over, "How is this possible that the Lord shows such great love for me, a sinner?" Because of a sad conflict with a parish priest, this otherwise good man had left the Church, but he felt great sorrow about it. And now he had proof that God had not abandoned him. His gratitude was so great that he seemed almost to forget his terrible pain, and death did not frighten him anymore.

Such astonishment and gratitude should not seem strange to us when we realize that God loves us sinners—so much so that he calls for our love in return.

This same astonishing and grateful love marked the whole life and activity of the Apostle to the Gentiles. Each new benefit and even each occasion to share in Christ's suffering reminded him of what a sinner he had been when the Lord chose and called him. These experiences increased his zeal for the glad tidings of reconciliation and helped him to bring many people to this same sense of marvel and of thankful love for Jesus.

Many of the Pharisees were shocked that Jesus showed such great love and kindness to "tax-collectors and other bad characters." They were scandalized and angry because it did not enter their minds that they, too, had no title whatsoever to be loved by God except through his own merciful love. Indeed, the arrogant conviction that one has deserving claims on God's love is one of the most serious sins against God's undeserved love for us: a sin that bars one's heart against this very love.

When the woman who was an object of public contempt began to show signs of sincere and humble love for Jesus, he welcomed that love, because it came from a contrite and grateful heart. And his acceptance gave her the hope that she could continue to grow in grateful and humble love. "Her great love proves that her many sins have been forgiven; where little has been forgiven, little love is shown" (Luke 7:47). This last assertion is a strong warning for those who think they are not really in need of divine mercy and forgiveness.

The saints are so touched by the healing love of God and so filled with awe before a God who loves sinners that they are scarcely tempted to weigh their own sins by looking down on others as greater sinners. Rather, they weigh their sins against the love of the all-holy God whom they have offended. Before him, our sins weigh against us in view of the many signs of grace by which he calls us to return his love. In the presence of God, any boast about personal merit is simply preposterous; there is place only for wonder and humble praise.

This wonder and praise mark the lives of the saints, particularly those who are great promoters of the devotion to the Sacred Heart of Jesus. We see it, for instance, in the prayers of St. Margaret Mary and, perhaps still more, in those of St. Alphonsus in his treatise *Novena to the Sacred Heart*. Like other theologians, St. Alphonsus speaks in his writings under the influence of grace. He was filled with amazement that God loves all people, even those who sin against him.

The contrition required for repentance is not just a vague kind of sorrow for our sins but a deep and painful grief for having offended a God who loves us so tenderly and mercifully. The word "mercy" (see the Latin *misericordia*) refers to a loving heart for those in misery, while the "miser" has no heart for those who are in need.

The marvel that God loves me, a sinner, forges the bonds of salvation-solidarity. If God loves me, how much must I then praise him for loving all of us who are sinners. Thus, we are joined in his praise and in mutual compassionate love.

Our tears of compassion in contemplating the unspeakable suffering of Jesus for sinners melts our pride and free us from fruitless self-pity. Our love response to Christ, crucified by us and for us, joins us in his compassion for all of us. If our hearts thus become conformed to the heart of Jesus, we are uniting ourselves with others as compassionate, warm-hearted, and generous disciples of Christ. Our gratitude and awe lead to zeal for the salvation of all.

This truth is touchingly expressed in the story of the calling and conversion of Levi (later called Matthew). As soon as Levi, the tax-gatherer, was called to follow Jesus in intimate friendship, he prepared for Jesus a festive meal to which he invited many other people like himself. "When Jesus was at table in his house, many bad characters—tax-gatherers and others—were seated with him and his disciples" (Mark 2:15), to the great scandal of some doctors of the law. Evidently, the humble heart of the newly converted Levi told him, "I am no better than other sinners. If the master invites me, then all are invited." Thus, Jesus celebrates the Messianic meal of the redeemed.

We find a similar example of awe and amazement in the text describing St. Peter's election. "Go, Lord, leave me, sinner that I am!" (Luke 5:8). Surely, Peter does not want to be abandoned by Jesus, but in his astonishment at being chosen, he realizes how unworthy he is of the friendship and nearness of Jesus. This event attains still greater depth and purification when, after his thrice-repeated denial of his Master, the risen Christ asks him three times about his friendship. Despite Peter's unworthiness, the Lord in his love confirms him as pastor in the steps of the Good Shepherd.

Holy Scripture gives other examples of how this humble amazement—that God calls "a sinner like me" to proclaim the salvation message—prepares a person to shoulder a difficult mission. At first, Isaiah cries out, "Woe is me! I am lost, for I am a man of unclean lips, and I dwell among a people of unclean lips; yet with these eyes I have seen the King, the Lord of Hosts" (Isaiah 6:5). But after being touched by the purifying fire of God's holy love, he hears the Lord saying, "Whom shall I send?" and he answers, "Here am I; send me" (Isaiah 6:8).

Second Isaiah foresees a totally new event in the "Servant of Yahweh" who alone is the One who is not surprised that "God loves me, a sinner." He is "One-of-us" but not a sinner. In him, God loves all sinners. Freely, he bears the burden of us all and leads us to the awesome truth that, in him and through him, God shows us so great a love. "Yet on himself he bore our sufferings, our torments he endured, while we counted him smitten by God, struck down by disease and misery; but he was pierced for our transgressions, tortured for our iniquities; the chastisement he bore is health for us and by his scourging we are healed" (Isaiah 53:4–5).

When we contemplate the pierced heart of Jesus, all discussions about who among us might be the greater sinner—or saint—are senseless. We can only unite in saying with awed amazement how tremendous must be the heart of God and his faithful Son and Servant to love us poor sinners! From this follows the "law of Christ" that we should all willingly bear each other's burdens. (See Galatians 6:2.)

Prayer

Saint Alphonsus' *Novena to the Sacred Heart*

Compassionate heart of Jesus, have mercy on me. I say it now, and give me the grace to say it always. Even before I offended you, I did not deserve to receive such great signs of your graciousness, O my Savior! You have created and enlightened me, all without any merit on my part. After offending you, I not only did not deserve your favor but also deserved to be abandoned by you. Yet, out of your compassionate love, you waited and conserved my life while I lived in disgrace. Your compassionate kindness has admonished me—inviting me to reconciliation—and has inspired in me contrition for my sins and the desire to love you.

And now, because of your mercy, I can hope to live in your grace. My Jesus, never stop showing me your favor. The mercy I ask is that you grant me light and strength never more to be ungrateful. I surely do not pretend that you are obliged to forgive me if I again turn away from you; this would be nothing less than presumption on my part and resistance to your compassionate love. It must never happen that I should ever again refuse your friendship. Dear Jesus, I love you, and I will always love you, and this is the mercy I hope for and humbly seek from you: let me never be separated from you!

Amen.

5

Late Did I Come to Love You

These are the words of the Lord: A people that survived the sword found favor in the wilderness; Israel journeyed to find rest; long ago the Lord appeared to them: I have dearly loved you from of old, and still I maintain my unfailing care for you. For I have become a father to Israel, and Ephraim is my eldest son....He who scattered Israel shall gather them again and watch over them as a shepherd watches his flock.

JEREMIAH 31:2–3, 9, 10

Show patience and a consistently gentle disposition toward all people. For at one time, we ourselves in our foolishness and stubbornness were all astray. We were slaves to passions and pleasures of every kind. Our days were passed in malice and envy; we were unhappy with ourselves and we hated one another. But when the kindness and generosity of God our Savior dawned upon the world, then, not for any good deeds of our own, but because he was merciful, he saved us through the water of rebirth and the renewing power of the Holy Spirit (Titus 3:2–5).

Even today, the words of St. Augustine of Hippo (354–430), "Late did I come to love you," speak to the hearts of many people who have gone through an experience similar to his. The phrase expresses both deep regret for so many years lost and, at the same time, grateful praise for the infinite forbearance and faithfulness of God. The personal experience of these people unites them with the People of God—which laments that so many of its members, in their individual and collective lives, have for a long time resisted God's grace and his appeal for total conversion and renewal. But the important point is that this sorrow, as indicated in Augustine's *Confessions*, inspires praise of God for his patience and for the final victory of his love.

We praise God, too, for the gift of so many saints, known and unknown to us, who have arrived at perfect love of God. When St. Teresa of Avila finally experienced God's unique love and became overwhelmed by it, she could only wonder with profound confusion how she could have lived a superficial life for so many years, despite all the opportunities for a better choice. If we consume our time with the trivial or lack the firm purpose and clear decision to make our hearts totally free for the Lord, we not only deprive ourselves of the joy of the Lord—the inner peace and the blissful experience of God's love for us—but we also impoverish the whole Church—indeed, the life of the world.

In most instances, ours will not be a matter of enslavement to destructive passions, as was the case with the young Augustine; rather, it will be the lack of firm decision to allow Christ to take hold of our whole being: our hearts, our minds, and our wills. Saint Alphonsus compares this attitude to that of an eagle who allows himself to be tied by a thin thread instead of breaking it and taking flight into the heights.

But the amazing truth is that, despite our shallowness, the Lord does not abandon us. He continues to gift us with an undivided love, time and again touching our hearts, a foretaste of the bliss that could be ours if only we would allow his love to conquer us fully.

It would be an unconscionable presumption to think that we have a certain right to our Lord's patience because we have shown occasional moments of fervor and have tried to avoid at least serious sin and scandal. This, in the midst of a superficiality that seduces us to give only second place to the love of God, surely does not entitle us to any kind of self-exaltation. In his treatise *Novena to the Sacred Heart*, St. Alphonsus offers a special meditation entitled "The Grateful Heart of Jesus," in which he praises the kindness of Jesus, who appreciates even our small steps toward full conversion and even our slightest efforts to please him. If Jesus treats us so kindly and patiently, it is all to the glory of the Father, with no merit on our part. We should be very much aware of this as an added motive for gratitude and generosity.

A profound grief for having lost so many precious years and so many unrepeatable opportunities to please God by serving the cause of his kingdom is a sign that God is gracious and continues to draw us to his heart. This grief, expressed in frequent prayers of thanksgiving, of praise, and of humble petition for a heart renewed, paves the way for the superabundant grace that God has prepared for us.

The firm decision to seek and to do, at all times and in all places, what pleases God must take deep roots in our hearts, our memories, and our wills, in our conscious and subconscious lives. Our motives and intentions must be purified and confirmed in the fire of the love of Jesus. No more time must be lost.

Prayer

The Confessions of Saint Augustine, Book 10

Late did I come to love you, O eternal and ever-new beauty; late, indeed, did I come to love you. You were within me, but I, like a bold intruder in your beautiful world, kept looking for you without. You were with me, but I was not with you. You called me; you cried out in a loud voice and finally overcame my deafness. You bathed me in your light, you wrapped me in your splendor, and you cured me of my blindness. You gave out a delightful fragrance, and I breathed it in and began to long for you. Having experienced your presence, I now hunger and thirst for you. You have touched me, and I burn to know your peace.

If I cling to you with all my heart, then I do not mind pain and toil. My life, if it is replete with you, is thoroughly alive.

But I myself, whom you lift up, am still a burden to myself, for I am not totally replete with you. My joys are mixed with tears, my smile with sadness. And still I am not sure to which side victory is inclining.

Look on me, O Lord; have mercy on me! There is still war between my evil afflictions and my good graces, and still I am not sure where victory lies. Lord, have mercy, look on my wounds. I do not try to conceal them. You are the physician; I am the patient. You are merciful; I am miserable.

All my hope is in your great mercy. Grant me what you command, and command what you will. O Love that ever glows and never is extinguished, O divine Love, my God, inflame me!

Amen.

6

Mary's Role in Her Son's Mission

[Jesus] was still speaking to the crowd when his mother and brothers appeared; they stood outside, wanting to speak to him. Someone said, "Your mother and your brothers are here outside; they want to speak to you." Jesus turned to the man who brought the message, and said, "Who is my mother? Who are my brothers?", and pointing to the disciples, he said, "Here are my mother and my brothers. Whoever does the will of my heavenly Father is my brother, my sister, my mother."

MATTHEW 12:46–50

MARY'S ROLE IN HER SON'S MISSION

The heart of Jesus, filled with love for us, is in a very special way near to his Mother. It was formed in her virginal womb, and there it began to beat in perfect harmony with her heart. The tender love of the most loving Mother on earth gave Jesus his first human experience of affection and dedication.

No doubt, since the first awakening of Jesus' consciousness, the unforgettable tenderness of his Mother's love was written in his heart. He would have understood well the prophet's word: "Can a woman forget the infant at her breast, or a loving mother the child of her womb? Even these forget, yet I will not forget you" (Isaiah 49:15).

Jesus' great mission was to reveal to us the love of God, our Father, through our understanding of human fatherly and motherly love and beyond it. In this mission, his Mother has a privileged role, first by communicating to Jesus a most tender and faithful motherly love, and then by joining him in the courageous and generous revelation of his love even up to the moment when she stood beneath his cross and saw him die.

A genuine devotion to the Sacred Heart of Jesus naturally includes devotion to the loving heart of Mary, his Mother and our Mother. We are grateful to her for the love she gave to Jesus, and we praise her for the love she received from him. She fulfilled for humanity her role as the new Eve, side by side with her Son.

Throughout her entire life, Mary is the Magnificat, an

everlasting praise of God, the all-merciful: "His mercy [is] sure from generation to generation" (Luke 1:50). John Paul II writes in his encyclical *Dives in Misericordia*, "No one has taken this mystery to heart as Mary has: this truly divine dimension of redemption wrought on Golgotha through the death of the Son of God, together with the sacrifice of her maternal heart, as shown in her definitive fiat."

We do not propose to overstress the psychic ties between Jesus and his Mother. Real as they were, they are not a determining factor in the incident quoted at the beginning of this chapter. Jesus had to detach himself from Nazareth, from his relatives, and even from his Mother for the sake of the "new family of God," of which he is the origin, and for total dedication to the Good News of the coming kingdom. This detachment is already prefigured by the decision of the twelve-year-old Jesus to remain in the temple while Mary and Joseph and the other pilgrims returned to their homes.

However, the detachment goes hand in hand with a new and stronger bond between the Son and his Mother, who, more so than anyone else, hears the Good News, keeps it in her heart, ponders over it, and puts it into practice. She is Jesus' first disciple, and she follows him all the way to Calvary.

In Luke's Gospel, when the humble, prophetic woman praises Jesus' Mother with the words, "Happy the womb that carried you and the breast that suckled you," Jesus turns his listeners' attention to what best distinguishes Mary and his new family: "No, happy are those who hear the Word of God and keep it" (Luke 11:27–28). The same gospel leaves no doubt that Mary is the outstanding model of this practice. (See Luke 2:19, 51.)

By continuing to preach the Good News while his Mother and brothers waited outside, Jesus taught us that in the "new family of God," spiritual relationships are more imposing than physical ones. But, again, he points implicitly to the outstanding model of these spiritual relationships: "Whoever does the will of my Father in heaven is my brother, my sister, my mother" (Matthew 12:50).

In the Father's design for the Redemption, Mary is uniquely privileged, and the love that Jesus shows her is also unique. With her, he rejoices in the praise of the heavenly Father; from her, he learned in his childhood Israel's songs of praise and, particularly, the songs of the Servant of Yahweh, which he made the program of his life. He knows his Mother to be "full of grace." In her, the Good News yields the richest and most precious harvest; she is a total "yes" to the will of God.

Hanging on the cross, Jesus turned to the "woman"—foretold in Genesis—whose offspring was to crush the head of the serpent. (See Genesis 3:15.) He entrusted to her the beloved disciple who represented all of us; at the same time, he entrusted the Mother to that same disciple. "And from that moment, the disciple took her into his home" (John 19:27). We, too, take her into our homes and our hearts if we have taken the Word of God into our hearts and keep it—even if, like Mary, we have to stand in the shadow of the cross.

Prayer

O my Savior, I praise you for the tender and faithful love that filled your heart even to the moment of its last pulsation on the cross. How much you have done to draw us all to you! Indeed, my heart is filled with joy when I remember that you compare your love for us poor sinners with your love for your holy Mother.

You assure us that we can be as near to your heart as she is if, with her, we join you in loving and doing the will of our heavenly Father. This is a mighty challenge and a powerful incentive for us to follow you in your total surrender to the loving will of the Father, even unto death. By this comforting and demanding word, you show us how wholly you were consecrated to the Father, so that we too, with Mary, your Mother, might be consecrated in truth. What more could you have done to spur us on to receive your word with grateful, loving hearts and to put it into practice! But if I examine closely the condition under which I may come as close to your heart as your Mother, then my mediocrity and superficiality make me angry with myself. What a fool I would be to jeopardize such a promise! Lord, forgive me; give me strength to renounce everything that hinders me on the road to this bliss. Help me always to hear your word and keep it—like your Mother!

Amen.

7

GOD'S LOVE IN REVELATION

The glory which thou gavest me, I have given to them, that they may be one, as we are one; I in them and thou in me, may they be perfectly one. Then the world will learn that thou didst send me, that thou didst love them as thou didst me. Father, I desire that these men, who are thy gift to me, may be with me where I am, so that they may look upon my glory, which thou hast given me because thou didst love me before the world began.…I made thy name known to them, and will make it known, so that the love thou hadst for me may be in them, and I may be in them.

JOHN 17:22–26

GOD'S LOVE IN REVELATION

In the Old Testament, God speaks to the hearts of the Israelites, using many startling images to emphasize his love for the chosen people. He loves Israel more than a father loves his darling child. His love is more tender than that of all mothers. His love is pictured, is likened, to the love between bridegroom and bride. No vinedresser is so careful of his vines as he is of his people. But all this good news is only a prelude to the full revelation of his love in Jesus Christ.

In the gospel, Jesus surprises us with totally unexpected sayings. "Whoever does the will of my heavenly Father is my brother, my sister, my mother" (Matthew 12:50). He allows us and invites us to call his Father "our Father." His unique relationship with the Father as the only begotten, eternal Son does not allow him to say that we are dear to him in the same way as his Father; yet, what he tells us about his disciples' share in that relationship surpasses anything that we might imagine. Here, we receive messages from Jesus that transform our hearts, our whole lives, and fill us with abiding joy if we receive them in faith.

Probably the most heartwarming texts are found in Jesus' farewell prayer, especially this one: "Then the world will learn that you love them as you love me," and this one that follows later: "So that the love you have for me may be in them, and I may be in them." Not only has the Father revealed his love in the loving heart of Jesus and given us Jesus as model, but he has, as it were, made the loving disciples of Christ, the true believers, a part of the love between the Father and Jesus.

In another heart-stirring message, Jesus says, "As the Father has loved me, so I have loved you" (John 15:9). The heart of Jesus, glowing with love for us, is here the "open port" through which he introduces us into the life of the triune God. We can respond only by adoring this mystery of God's astonishing self-revelation.

If, as believers and loving disciples of Jesus, we join him in his "Abba, dear Father," then the Holy Spirit is the One who prays in us and enables us to say this so truthfully that it will mark all of our lives and all of our relationships (See Romans 8:15; Galatians 4:6): "Because God's love has flooded our inmost heart through the Holy Spirit he has given us" (Romans 5:5).

In his high-priestly prayer, Jesus expresses four times the blissful message that he considers his disciples as special gifts of the Father and that, therefore, they are dear to his heart. "I pray for them…for those whom you have given me, because they belong to you. All that is mine is yours, and what is yours is mine, and through them has my glory shone" (John 17:9–10). Jesus knows that he has been sent for us (John 17:3, 8,18, 21, 23, 25). It follows that Jesus and those who cling to him in faith are gifts of the Father for each other in an indescribable exchange. What greater incentive could there ever be to love Jesus, to love with him the Father, and to love with the Father and Jesus all of God's children?

In the name of Jesus, whom the Father has given us, we can pray with unlimited trust. But this name leads us to pray, above all, that we may receive grateful love for him and the Father. Time and again, with ever-increasing awe and amazement, we will meditate on the truth that, as believers, we can love the heavenly Father with the love of Jesus and, in return, love Jesus with the love of the Father. Thus, immersed in the life of the Father, the Son, and the Holy Spirit, we can love each other, accept each other, and honor each other as gifts from the Father.

This, then, is a life's program offered to us by Jesus when, speaking "heart to heart" with the Father, he takes us, his disciples, most wonderfully into this dialogue. In this exchange of love, we join with the heart of Jesus, which, glowing with love for his Father and all humanity, is ready to manifest his love and trust, even on the cross. With him, we entrust ourselves to the Father and his loving will, though we might not yet understand it in all its dimensions.

Being at home with Jesus and the Father in the abiding love of the Spirit, we begin to grasp the beauty of our mission: "As the Father has loved me, so I have loved you. Dwell in my love. Love one another as I have loved you" (John 15:9, 12).

Prayer

Our dear Savior, when you spoke heart to heart with your heavenly Father, you made your disciples—indeed all believers—an intimate part of this interchange of love and trust. I would never dare to feel included if the disciples who were present there had been spotless and blameless. You chose them when they were still unlike you. You knew they would fail you at the time of your ordeal, yet you took them wholly into that wonderful exchange with the Father. Thus, I, a sinner, can dare to think that I too was included. O, wonder of wonders!

We praise you, Father, Lord of heaven and earth, for having revealed in Jesus your great love for us together with your love for your only Son. Through his loving heart, you have shown us the way to your heart's inmost mystery of love. The One you have sent tells us, "He who loves me will be loved by my Father; and I will love him and disclose myself to him. Anyone who loves me will heed what I say; then my Father will love him, and we will come to him and make our dwelling with him" (John 14:21–23). This assurance reminds me to pay no attention to my own desires. All else pales before this blissful light, and at the same time, all that is good, true, and beautiful shines forth in your light. Everything is your gift, and all your gifts call us to love you.

Your supreme and all-encompassing gift to us is

Jesus, in whom the fullness of the Godhead dwells and in whom and through whom you share with us your own love. This unsurpassable gift assures us that, if we pray faithfully, you will give a second gift: new hearts that will be able to love you and Jesus worthily, hearts filled with your Spirit and overflowing with generosity and kindness for all of your children. Now and always, I shall beg you to grant us this love, these new hearts. Now and forever, let us be at home in the heart of Jesus, so that we may love you with his love.

Amen.

8

ONLY LOVE
COUNTS

*I may speak in tongues of men or of angels,
but if I am without love, I am a sounding gong
or a clanging cymbal. I may have the gift of
prophecy, and know every hidden truth; I may
have faith strong enough to move mountains;
but if I have no love, I am nothing.
I may dole out all I possess, or even give my body
to be burnt, but if I have no love, I am none the
better.*

1 CORINTHIANS 13:1–3

God is Love, and all his works and words are the overflow and revelation of his love. The supreme manifestation of his love for us sinful people is that he sent us his only Son, who, in loving obedience to the mandate of his Father, gave himself up totally for us. If we study all of God's work but remain unmindful of his love, we completely miss the mark. Indeed, we would miss God himself. Not only would the deepest meaning and beauty remain concealed from us, but, without the code of love, we could not rightly decipher God's loving will regarding his various works and gifts.

Surely, God requests good deeds from us, but not as our own boastful achievements, not as something done without love or as works done for the wrong reasons. What matters is love itself, offered with all our hearts and all our strength, in response to God's love for us. What really counts is the love of people who are so imbued with God's love that its fruits arise from their innermost being. Only thus are we "in the truth"—created images of the eternal Word that breathes Love, the Holy Spirit, the "Spirit of Truth." By its very nature, such love is fruitful, having its deep roots in Jesus' shared love for us.

This is the marvelous vision granted us by John's Gospel: "He who dwells in me, as I dwell in him, bears much fruit; for apart from me, you can do nothing. If you dwell in me, and my words dwell in you, ask what you will, and you shall have it. This is my Father's glory, that you may bear fruit in plenty and so be my disciples" (John 15:5, 7–8).

Here, we touch one of the essential points of the devotion to the Sacred Heart. If, lovingly, we make our abiding home in the heart of Jesus and entrust ourselves completely to him, we discover that we can love resolutely with heart and hands, with memory, intellect, and affections. We can trustfully embrace our mission. By the love that flows from the heart of Jesus, our intellect becomes lucid, sensitive, alert. A heart inflamed and seized by Christ's love shapes the will to choose what is good.

Already in the Old Testament, this was the peak of revelation. God, the Revealer and Redeemer, speaks to the hearts of his people: "What then, O Israel, does the Lord your God ask of you? Only to fear the Lord your God, to conform to all his ways, to love him and to serve him with all your heart and soul" (Deuteronomy 10:12).

By fulfilling the Old Testament prophecies, Jesus tells us that this all-encompassing commandment can be obeyed by the redeemed who trust in his grace. He takes us by the hand and introduces us into the beauties of his love and of a life totally dedicated to this love. Those who are devoted to the heart of Jesus must prepare to take three giant steps: first, learn how to love Jesus and the Father in heaven; secondly, learn what it means to love—with Jesus and "in Jesus"—our neighbor and all those loved by him; and third, pray unceasingly for the gift of the Spirit who breathes love into our hearts and grants us the discernment to distinguish between redeemed love and its counterfeits.

In this learning process, it is important to see clearly how our love response embraces and includes all virtues and all divine commandments. Each of these, just as love itself, are gracious gifts of God. Here, we come face to face with the central task of Christian education and moral theology that "love alone counts," which is a part of our best Catholic tradition.

How poor are those children whose parents give them a thousand things but are unable or unwilling to give themselves, their hearts, love, affirmation, and time! A happy father of seven childre told me this story: "After the Christmas holidays, there was a family get-together at our home. The children of the other family members began boasting about the many expensive gifts they had received. After a moment of silence, a surprising comment came from my ten-year-old Elisabeth. To these boastful children, each of whom was an 'only' child, she replied, 'Our gifts are Joseph, John, Francis, Antonia, Agatha, Catherine—and whom have you?' It was a revelation from a child's heart and lips about what true wealth is."

Christian obedience derives its meaning and purpose from the freedom to love, to care, to affirm one's neighbor. The exercise of authority in caring for the common good becomes the response to the way Christ was obedient and, at the same time, an embodiment of prophetic freedom.

In this sense, St. Ignatius of Loyola gives meaning to his motto, "Everything for the greater glory of God," through loving conformity with Christ. "When it is a matter of discerning what equally might be for the greater glory of God, I look at Christ and how I can follow him most intimately and become more like him. Therefore, I love and prefer poverty with Christ rather than riches. I prefer to be insulted with Christ rather than to be honored. I prefer to be considered an insignificant man and a fool for Christ's sake rather than to be praised as wise and clever in this world." Such a choice makes sense only for loving hearts.

Prayer

Lord Jesus Christ, full of love and worthy of all love, you are the Father's greatest gift to us. You not only offer us countless precious gifts, you give yourself with all your love. You open for us the treasures of your loving heart, and it is this heart's love that gives all your gifts an infinite value. Through them, you speak to our hearts.

What thanks can I offer you in return, Lord Jesus, except my heartfelt love? And, as another wonderful gift, you let me know that you accept it for no other reason than that of your own love for me, which is the motivation for my response.

But how could I have dared, during so many years, to offer you no more than a superficial, divided, and inconsistent love? A thousand times I have deserved to hear you say that you refuse to accept such a mixture of good and not-so-good motives. It is only your merciful love that moved you to look graciously on my yearning to purify my affections and find a way to love you better. For this very purpose, you have allowed suffering and pressure to afflict me; you have given me insight and strength to help me learn in the school of suffering. You are showing me the way to gather all this together in a prayer of thanksgiving. Yes, Lord, I know that in all things you work tenderly to purify my heart and to conquer it for your blessed friendship.

Lord, I am beginning to understand that only love can be my proper response to you—a love that comes from you and leads to you. From now on—until my last breath and my last heartbeat—I shall pray for nothing more than the grace to love you with all my heart, all my soul, all my strength. Increase this yearning so that I may become ever more ready to receive this greatest gift.

Amen.

9

OUR FAILURE TO LOVE

I will sing for my beloved
my love-song about his vineyard:
My beloved had a vineyard high up on a fertile
hillside.
He trenched it and cleared it of stones and planted it
with red vines;
he built a watchtower in the middle and then hewed
out a winepress in it.
He looked for it to yield grapes,
but it yielded wild grapes.
Now, you who live in Jerusalem, and you men of
Judah,
judge between me and my vineyard.
What more could have been done for my vineyard
that I did not do in it?
The vineyard of the Lord of Hosts is Israel,
and the men of Judah are the plant he cherished.

ISAIAH 5:1–4, 7

OUR FAILURE TO LOVE

The Old Testament prophets rightfully saw Israel's refusal to love God faithfully as a shocking and frightening event. God himself complains, through the prophetic voices, about this thanklessness of hardened hearts. He asks his chosen people, "What more could I have done for you?"

This question becomes even more heart-rending in today's world. We see the heart of Jesus opened for us and his blood shed for us, yet so many have refused to love this God who has done wondrous things to reveal his love and to touch our hearts. Observing, on one hand, the overflowing love of the heart of Jesus and, on the other, the lack of love on humanity's part, many saints have cried out in pain: "The greatest Love is not loved!"

It is alarming to see fulfilled among so many Christians the prophecy that "men's love for one another will grow cold" (Matthew 24:12). No wonder that our love for one another grows cold when we do not care to respond even to God's own love for us! We cut ourselves off from the source of all love.

How terribly the heart of Jesus must have been afflicted when he saw how quickly the ardor of many in the crowds who had listened to him and had experienced his healing love and power had grown cold! He saw even his beloved disciples abandon him. All this foreshadowed for Jesus what would happen throughout history.

The liturgy ascribes to Jesus this and similar laments: "I

looked for consolation and received none, for comfort and did not find any" (Psalm 69:20). Our devotion to the Sacred Heart returns again and again to the same theme. This is one of the striking dimensions in the religious experience of St. Margaret Mary Alacoque. And the hearts of believers are deeply moved when on Good Friday they hear in the Reproaches: "My people, what have I done to you? How have I offended you? Answer me!"

If we truly have believing and sensitive hearts, of necessity we are deeply troubled by this devastating lovelessness that assails the heart of Jesus, pierced for us first by the soldier's lance and pierced again in every generation by the steel-cold hearts of so many people.

Jesus' pain arises, above all, from the offense and insult given to his heavenly Father by our unjustifiable refusal to love him despite the full revelation of his love for us. He also sees the disastrous consequences of the mindless ingratitude of those who close their hearts to saving love and who poison their environment by their heartless "no." It is, indeed, a senseless act of destruction directed against the noblest potentialities of the human person, who is still called to find his or her perfection and joy in thankful response to God's love. How can Jesus not be pained by this foolish rebellion against one's self and surroundings, when thankful love would have created a new person and a new environment radiating peace?

Whoever refuses to return God's love becomes, by this

very injustice, guilty of further injustice against fellow human beings—a source of lovelessness, frustration, deception. Such a one becomes a slave and makes others slaves of the "sin of the world," of solidarity in evil. If I sin, it is always due to a lack of love for God on my part; this, in turn, decreases my capacity to love him, my neighbor, and myself with a true love. I thus become a partial cause of a growing coldness of heart in the world. My sin strikes back not only against me but also against the common good. One who refuses God's love is choosing, instead, to bear the heavy burden of collective sinfulness in all its forms.

This reflection is a dominant factor in our devotion to the Sacred Heart when it comes from a heart touched by the all-embracing love of Jesus. If our reflection is authentic, it will lead to a deep and liberating sorrow and a burning desire to offer Jesus and the Father the satisfaction of true love. It will also lead to an active compassion toward all people who are lukewarm and foster a desire in them to strive to love God with all their heart.

John, the beloved disciple, standing beneath the cross, witnessed the fateful scene when the soldier pierced the heart of Jesus with his lance. He quotes the Scripture that this event fulfilled, presuming that we will be mindful of it: "They shall look on him whom they pierced" (John 19:37). Thus, he turns our attention, our memory, our eyes, and our hearts to this heart pierced for us, and he expects us to remember that our sins were among those that wounded the heart of Jesus. For us, as loving, grateful, and repentant believers, these thoughts should produce both a deep sorrow for our sins and grief for all human sins; at the same time, it should inflame our hearts with a fervent and faithful love. The Old Testament text recalled by John expresses best the fruits of such a loving contemplation: "I will pour a spirit of pity and compassion into the line of David and the inhabitants of Jerusalem. Then they shall look on me, on him whom they have pierced" (Zechariah 12:10).

The lives of many saints tell us how the shock of seeing such a meager response to the boundless love of God, coupled with the grateful remembrance of the heart of Jesus pierced by us and for us, can produce a profound change of our hearts, minds, wills, and fundamental relationships—indeed, of our whole lives.

Prayer

Loving heart of Jesus, you chose poverty on earth so that nothing could conceal the wealth of the love that you offer us. Freely, you embraced all the turmoil, all the fatigue and risks of a homeless preacher, to proclaim everywhere that the kingdom of Love is at hand. You gathered disciples around you to let them feel the warmth of your friendship, the tenderness of your healing and redeeming love.

Not only with words did you teach us that "there is

no greater love than this, that a man should lay down his life for his friends" (John 15:13). With the paramount purpose of revealing the height and depth, the length and breadth of your love and that of the Father, you have stretched out your arms for us on the cross. You have allowed the lance to pierce your heart and have given for us the last drop of your most precious blood. Surely, if anyone does not love you and your heavenly Father, there is no excuse. Lord Jesus, it pains me to know that so many people do not care at all for your love but prefer to remain slaves to a destructive self-love and to individual and collective egotism. Even more painful is the thought that many of those who had begun to rejoice in your love have violated their commitment to you and have turned to poisoned cisterns, refusing you, the source of living water.

It is shocking to learn that even priests and religious have abandoned their first love and act as if they never had known you. But the most piercing pain for me is to realize that I, too, have withheld a part of my love while squandering much of it. Faced with the sad fact that the love of many is growing cold, I beg you to inflame my heart wholly with your love and send me to win over the hearts of many for your love.

Amen.

10

Heart of Jesus, Healer of Our Hearts

I kneel in prayer to the Father, from whom every family in heaven and on earth takes its name, that out of the treasures of his glory he may grant you strength and power through his Spirit in your inner being; that through faith, Christ may dwell in your hearts in love. With deep roots and firm foundations, may you be strong to grasp, with all God's people, what is the breadth and length and height and depth of the love of Christ, and to know it, though it is beyond knowledge. So may you attain to fullness of being, the fullness of God himself.

EPHESIANS 3:14–19

Mark embodies the preaching of Jesus in these words: "The time has come; the kingdom of God is upon you; repent, and believe the Gospel" (Mark 1:15). The Greek word that we translate as either "repent" or "be converted" is *metanoeite*. It means a whole new way of thinking, feeling, longing: a new heart. We could translate it as "be renewed in your heart." The good news is that now the promised time has come when God himself, by the power of the Spirit, will create in us a new heart. "I will…bring you to your own soil. I will sprinkle clean water over you, and you shall be cleansed from all that defiles you; I will cleanse you from the taint of all your idols. I will give you a new heart and put a new spirit within you; I will take the heart of stone from your body and give you a heart of flesh. I will put my Spirit into you" (Ezekiel 36:24–26; see also Jeremiah 31:34).

This wondrous healing cannot happen through a mere imperative of new laws and external structures in our world. It happens through faith: we allow the Good News to take hold of us, and we entrust ourselves totally to God, who, in Jesus, opens the treasures of his love for us. In this way, God writes his grace and law into our hearts. (See Jeremiah 31:33.) Eye to eye and heart to heart with Jesus, we become new people. We think, feel, yearn, and love differently. We see God through the eyes of grateful love. We arrive at a knowledge of the good—of what is good, true, and beautiful, accessible only to a heart renewed in love.

Those holy people who venerated the Sacred Heart through the centuries communicate this truth in various ways. St. John Henry Newman, for instance, is inspired by the image of St. John reposing on Jesus' heart. He speaks of the disciple's longing for a perfect love of Jesus, "until heart in heart repose" and "heart speaks to heart." Others speak of the "arrow of love" coming from Jesus' heart and piercing our heart. It is a flame of love that wounds and, at the same time, heals the heart. Some speak of an "exchange of hearts" offered by Jesus himself to those who yearn for his love.

Saint Augustine calls Jesus the "joy of the pure heart" in the same sense that Jesus calls "blessed" those whose hearts are pure: "they shall see God" (Matthew 5:8). Touched and purified, they now see with "eyes of love." For St. Paul, this means that "through faith, Christ may dwell in your hearts in love" (Ephesians 3:17). Justification and sanctification are the work of grace through faith bearing fruit in love. By knowing God "with the heart," we are configured to the heart of Jesus, who wants us "to be without blemish in his sight" (Ephesians 1:4).

In Holy Scripture, the word heart frequently means a conscience sensitive to God's calling and to everything that is good; a conscience guided and illumined by love. For the Christian, this means knowing Jesus lovingly and considering everything in the sight of God. It implies the exercise of saving solidarity by those whose hearts have been won by the love of the Redeemer. With this new heart, we arrive at higher levels of discernment. We begin to think as members of the family of God.

All this powerful attraction and transformation is grace, insertion into the life of Christ. Jesus tells us, "No man can come to me unless he is drawn by the Father who sent me" (John 6:44). "No one knows who the Son is but the Father, or who the Father is but the Son, and those to whom the Son may choose to reveal him" (Luke 10:22). Entering the realm of truth and love through the portal of Jesus' heart, being at home in this loving heart, reposing beside Jesus, the disciple develops a new kind of conscience. Everything appears in a new light and has new beauty. Every virtue and every law of God acquires its proper place in the whole picture and becomes attractive. One's conscience thus becomes alert for the signs of the times, for what the present hour offers, and for the many opportunities to give testimony for Christ and his reign.

This change of heart and conscience can be seen in the light of Jesus' word: "Come to me all whose work is hard, whose load is heavy and I will give you relief. Bend your necks to my yoke, and learn from me, for I am gentle and humble-hearted; and your souls will find relief. For my yoke is good to bear, my load is light" (Matthew 11:28–30).

The assault of our passions, slavish fear, and anguish ceases when we repose near the heart of Jesus. We feel new strength, new joy in doing God's will, acknowledging it not as a law imposed but as an invitation to live as beloved and loving children, as intimate friends. And, as a result, the decisions of our conscience become more confident, creative, and generous.

In accord with the biblical meaning of "heart," we may also say that reposing in Jesus' heart affects even our unconscious—and our subconscious—life. Not even the best psychotherapists can liberate our conscious and subconscious psychic life as surely as does a new heart-to-heart relationship with Jesus. Absorbed in the love of Jesus, a grateful memory opens new avenues for grasping present opportunities, for reshaping past tendencies, and for opening creative doors into the future.

For those who live closest to the heart of Jesus, this transformation of conscience will lead not only to some courageous decisions after a hard fight against the "old Adam" present in everyone but also to an ever more ready response to their neighbors' needs, and in a way that radiates joy and peace.

Jesus warns us, "What comes out of the mouth has its origins in the heart" (Matthew 15:18); he also says, "The words that the mouth utters come from the overflowing heart" (Matthew 12:34). We also remember the words: "Where your treasure is, there will your heart be also" (Matthew 6:21). The "formation of conscience" by laws and precepts, and even by criteria for discernment, is one thing; quite another, and much further-reaching and fruitful, is formation of the depth-conscience in a heart-to-heart friendship with Jesus.

Those who, in all things, seek first the kingdom of God, whose hearts beat with the heart of Jesus in a love that surpasses all imagination, are best prepared for seeking and finding what is good, truthful, and beautiful. Drawn by the love of Christ, the depth-conscience, like a magnetic needle, will point to a clear orientation of life.

The insights of depth psychology about the great importance of our unconscious and subconscious forces are far from being a denial of freedom. Quite the contrary! If we learn to heal our memories, to fill them with thankfulness and loving attention, if we allow Jesus to conquer our hearts for his love and for loving our neighbor with him, our "soul will find relief" and we will move toward a truly "hearty" health and a new freedom for trust and love.

Prayer

St. John Henry Newman

O my dear Lord, I need thee to teach me day by day, according to each day's opportunities and needs. I need thee to give me a true divine instinct about revealed matters. Give me the gift of discerning between true and false in all discourse of mind. And for that end, give me that purity of conscience that alone can receive, that alone can profit by thine inspirations.

My ears are dull, so that I cannot hear thy voice. My eyes are dim, so that I cannot see thy gifts of grace. Thou alone can quicken my hearing, purge my sight, and cleanse and renew my heart. Teach me, like Mary, to sit at thy feet and hear thy word.

Give me that true wisdom that seeks thy will by prayer and meditation, by direct communication with thee more than by reading and reasoning.

I believe, O my Savior, that thou loves me better than I love myself. I know thou will do thy part toward me, as I, through thy grace, desire to do my part toward thee. I know well thou can never abandon those who seek thee or cannot disappoint those who trust in thee.

Keep me ever from being afraid of thine eye, from the inward consciousness that I am not honestly trying to please thee.

Teach me to love thee more, and then I shall be at peace, without any fear of thee at all.

And at the place thou hast assigned me, I shall be a messenger of thy peace.

Amen.

11

ONLY LOVE CAN ATONE

Fortitude you have; you have borne up in my cause and never flagged. But I have this against you: you have lost your early love. Think from what a height you have fallen; repent, and do as once you did.

REVELATION 2:3–5

These are the words of the Son of God, whose eyes flame like fire and whose feet gleam like burnished brass: I know all your ways, your love and faithfulness, your good service and your fortitude; and of late you have done even better than at first.

REVELATION 2:19

ONLY LOVE CAN ATONE

Having considered how greatly God has loved us and how ungrateful has been our response, it is time now to speak of atonement, which, in the official devotion to the Sacred Heart, plays an important role. But for various reasons, many people never reach this stage. Some, ignoring the basic purpose of atonement, see it only as cruel mortification and extreme reparation. Others reject the devotion outright because of these or other misinterpretations.

At the beginning of their conversion, many holy people, including Blessed Henry Suso, the great propagator of the devotion to the Sacred Heart, imposed on themselves cruel chastisements, even to the detriment of health; however, at a certain point, the Lord gave them the insight that he does not want this kind of atonement. Blessed Henry was then taught to atone by heartfelt love, unlimited trust, and total conformity to the loving will of God. In a similar way, St. Margaret Mary Alacoque came to the same understanding. While Jansenistic[1] nuns of her time insisted on difficult external penances, this humble nun relayed the message of the Sacred Heart that love alone counts for atonement. From deep sorrow for our own sins and for the grievous

---

[1] The heresy of "Jansenism," as stated by subsequent Roman Catholic doctrine, lies in the denial of the role of free will in the acceptance and use of grace. Jansenism asserts that God's role in the infusion of grace cannot be resisted and does not require human assent. The *Catechism of the Catholic Church (CCC)* states the Roman Catholic position that "God's free initiative demands man's free response" (*CCC* 2002), that is, humans are said to freely assent or refuse God's gift of grace.

lack of love offered to God who is Love, there must arise an insatiable desire to atone by a pure and fervent love for Jesus and—thus united with Jesus "unto death"—to offer satisfaction to the Father.

The first question about atonement, therefore, cannot be what kind of suffering we should inflict upon ourselves. We should not afflict ourselves at all with useless suffering. Rather, the question is how to achieve that great love that atones for our earlier lack of love and for the refusal of love by which so many people offend God. We must yearn and pray for this love, because it is an unmerited gift of God, and then accept all the sacrifices needed to express our love in the service of our brothers and sisters.

Saint Augustine describes the history of salvation and, indeed, the history of the world as a relentless battle between two kinds of love: pure, strong, and grateful love of God, which engenders a redeemed and redeeming love of neighbor, and a perverted self-love.

The first step to atoning love is to strive faithfully to attain the purification of our love at any cost. As Pope Pius XI writes, the veneration of the Sacred Heart implies "a repentant love" and a "love attentive to satisfaction." He explains that this special kind of love calls for a simple lifestyle and a covenant to make sacrifices that are indispensable if we are to manifest an effective love for those in need. In other words, atonement, as a part of our devotion to the Sacred Heart, does not mean sacrifices in addition to love but sacrifices that are the requirements of love itself. This is an indispensable condition for the purification, growth, and manifestation of true love.

Those famous mystical theologians of the eleventh and twelfth centuries, who were among the great venerators of the Sacred Heart, emphasized that Jesus alone could atone, because our love, being weak and insufficient, cannot be offered to the Father as atonement. For them, this called for a particularly grateful love for the Sacred Heart, a fruitful love that would include the readiness to join Christ on his road to Calvary.

Quite different was the emphasis that derives from the spirituality of St. Francis of Assisi and St. Catherine of Siena. They place in the foreground the configuration with Christ, especially in his compassion. Jesus has offered, in the name of humanity, such a fullness of atonement that derived from it is an atoning value of the love of his disciples united with his passion and compassion.

That Jesus has atoned in the name of humanity does not dispense his followers from atonement. Rather, it enables and obliges us to realize in our own lives what Christ has offered in our name, the name of humanity. It is this atoning love of ours that is still missing and is desired for the glory of the Father, for our own good and for the common good of the redeemed. This way of looking on our atoning vocation is part and parcel of the religious experiences of St. Margaret Mary. It is also the official interpretation of this devotion by the Church's teaching authority and as seen in the liturgy.

This perspective is offered by the Apostle to the Gentiles: "It is now my happiness to suffer for you. This is my way of helping to complete, in my poor human flesh, the full tale of Christ's afflictions still to be endured, for the sake of his body which is the Church" (Colossians 1:24). Christ has given evidence of his atoning love in all his life and in his passion and death. His love is so great that all his manifestations of love for the Father have absolute, infinite value. Yet he went all the way to the supreme test on the cross. Insofar as Christ acted as the head of the Church, there can be nothing lacking. But what is still to be completed is the appropriation of this same love by his disciples, tested by their readiness to bear the cross with Christ. His atoning love, made in the name of the Church, has to become embodied in the Church, for the sake of humanity.

In view of the overflowing redemption in Christ, every member of the Church should concentrate on loving atonement. One who receives redemption and refuses to become an active, responsive member of the body of Christ deprives oneself of the dynamics of redemption and deprives the Church and the world of one's share in a redemptive solidarity. This pertains to the very substance of the doctrine that "in him is plentiful redemption."

And it should be made quite clear that atonement becomes meritorious not because of the amount of our mortifications and reparation but because of the depth, strength, and purity of our love. The message of the Book of Revelation to the "angel of Ephesus" acknowledges that the community has borne much turmoil for the sake of Christ yet reproaches it ("You have lost your early love"), whereas Thyatira receives approbation because "of late you have done even better than at first." (See 2:4, 19.)

Prayer

Dear Lord and Master, I thank you and hope to be allowed to thank you in all eternity for your great love by which you have atoned for our sins and offered a worthy reparation to our heavenly Father.

Despite all the misery and sin in the world, we can rejoice, for from this earth—from our human frailty—the Father has received, through you, the most perfect response of love and loving atonement. We thank you for having done this in our name—in the name of all of us sinners. For us, it is a great blessing that by your loving atonement you have shamed and challenged us for our lack of true love.

What value could my suffering and turmoil have if they were offered to the heavenly Father without your previous offering? And how could I ever dare to offer my weak and confused love to the all-holy God as atonement for my own and other people's sins if it had not received its real value from your atonement and love for us?

Dear Savior, I thank you for giving me a home in your loving heart and accepting my love—offered in union with yours—in atonement to the Father.

We praise you, dear Redeemer, for by your earthly life and your bitter passion you have given value to our repentant love and to the sufferings that we accept in order to thank you and praise you. Keep us always united with you. Help us to grow in your love, so that the Father can see you present in our efforts to purify our love and make it a sign of loving atonement.

Amen.

12

ATONING VALUE OF SUFFERING

In Jesus, however, we do see one…crowned now with glory and honor because he suffered death, so that, by God's gracious will, in tasting death he should stand for us all.

It was clearly fitting that God, for whom and through whom all things exist, should, in bringing many sons to glory, make the leader who delivers them perfect through sufferings. For a consecrating priest and those whom he consecrates are all of one stock, and that is why the Son does not shrink from calling men his brothers, when he says…"Here am I, and the children whom God has given me."…And therefore he had to be made like these brothers of his in every way, so that he might be merciful and faithful as their high priest before God, to expiate the sins of the people.

HEBREWS 2:9–17

Son though he was, he learned obedience in the school of suffering, and, once perfected, became the source of eternal salvation for all who obey him.

HEBREWS 5:8–9

ATONING VALUE OF SUFFERING

One day in the concentration camp at Auschwitz, when the guards had been unusually cruel, a desperate prisoner cried out to God, "Where are you now?" But from the opposite corner of the room, another prisoner answered in a loud voice, "Don't you see him, crucified here again, hanging on his cross?" This unusual dialogue between sufferers sheds much light on how the heart of Jesus schools us in suffering and also enlightens us on the meaning of atonement. Jesus' suffering reveals an essential dimension of atonement for our sins—but how and why, no human tongue will ever be able to explain. It remains an unfathomable mystery that God should plunge so deeply into the suffering of a sinful world and expose himself, in his Son, even to calumny and torture by men.

This profound mystery is symbolized in the Sacred Heart of Jesus. Pope Pius XII wrote in his encyclical *Haurietis Aquas*, "Without penetrating into the mystical depths of Jesus' heart, no one ever fittingly loves the Crucified." Conversely, we may also say that no one can be taken by Jesus into the mystical depths of his heart unless he or she is ready to express love and gratitude to Jesus by sharing his suffering.

In the history of theology, we find many efforts to approach the mystery of atonement through Jesus. No one theory is satisfactory, because the mystery is beyond human reason. We can only conjecture as we investigate this divine secret from various starting points.

The Letter to the Hebrews, quoted at the beginning of this chapter, does give us some special insights. It is not the author's point at all that only such extreme suffering could fully atone for our sins. The key is, rather, that it was "fitting"—in the divine plan of salvation—that the Son of God, made man for our salvation, "One-of-us" in all things except sin, should also and in the fullest measure share in our suffering.

The logic of divine love and of the heart of Jesus is not, primarily, that we should also suffer because Jesus suffered so much. No, it is much loftier than that: because humanity, having burdened itself with sin, was inevitably exposed to all kinds of suffering, our Redeemer and Brother Jesus did not want to avoid suffering himself. Indeed, he, the God-Man with the most sensitive heart and mind, suffered more than anyone else. But what has redeemed us is not suffering as such but suffering as manifestation of the greatest love. Thus, Jesus taught us to transform suffering, to give it a new meaning of liberating love. And with this "new meaning," our understanding deepens. Because Jesus has suffered so much for us, it is "fitting" that his disciples also say "yes" to their suffering and take it as a sign of an all-embracing solidarity and of grateful love for Jesus, who shows us the way.

A solidarity in sin makes others suffer senselessly, while a saving solidarity in Christ bears the burden of others. Hence, we accept meaningful suffering and make meaningful the suffering that otherwise would be meaningless.

ATONING VALUE OF SUFFERING

It is in this way that we enter the life-giving stream of salvation, into the redemptive work of Jesus. Accepting and sharing in this stream of human and divine love in the heart of Jesus, we become a part of redeeming solidarity.

The Letter to the Hebrews boldly says that Jesus, "Son though he was, learned obedience in the school of suffering" (5:8). Even before suffering, from the first moment of human consciousness, he was all loving obedience to the heavenly Father. He had total trust in the Father's love and wisdom. But to be fully "One-of-us" and to show us the way, he wanted also to learn by the deepest experience what trusting, loving obedience is in the midst of the most intense suffering. What this indicates is not how much we have to suffer but how great was his love—bringing, as it did, this redemptive and efficacious meaning to suffering.

The cruelest human suffering with which people afflict each other comes from the lack of love in their hearts. Nobody was as worthy of endless love as Jesus was, yet nobody has been afflicted with such lovelessness. He has shown us how to take the poison out of such suffering; he has taught us to break the vicious circle of pain and to sanctify it by the most forgiving and healing love. And he has shown this greatest love not only for his friends by giving his life for them, but he has done the same even for his enemies who crucified him. He died for us, who, by our sins, have behaved as enemies. Yet, for all of us, Jesus prays, "Father, forgive!"

His heart is physically pierced by the soldier's lance after being painfully pierced by humanity's loveless offenses—by friends who should have stood beneath the cross with Mary and the beloved disciple, consoling him with grateful love.

Even by our lesser sins, which sometimes cause serious wounds to ourselves and others, we also wound the heart of Jesus, even though we do not completely turn away from him. The sensitive heart of Jesus was wounded not only by those who slandered him while he was hanging on the cross but also by those who had known him and disinterestedly stayed away. We wound the body of Christ and the heart of Christ by so many sins of omission!

We should be mindful of all this if we wish to attend the Jesus school of suffering. There, we should never cease thanking him for giving a new meaning to suffering and enabling us to do the same. Safe in his love, we praise him for calling us to share actively in his work of redemption.

Faith, prompted by the power of the Spirit, is a gift flowing from the heart of Jesus. It is essential for a living faith that in our sufferings and trials we entrust ourselves to Jesus, to the "thoughts of God's heart." Even the worst sufferings—those caused by our own sins or foolishness—are lightened if we confidently believe that for those who love God, everything will turn out all right. It is also consoling to know that if our sufferings are accepted with faith and love, Jesus will make of them a fountain of grace for others—with their meaning transfigured by his own suffering, they flow from his heart, the fountain of all grace.

The sufferings of believers who dwell "in Christ," especially of those who are persecuted for the sake of faith and justice, are a part of the sufferings of the Church. It is the Church who, by sharing in the passion of Christ, prepares itself for "the wedding-supper of the Lamb" (Revelation 19:9) and, indeed, has already begun to celebrate the eternal wedding feast.

Jesus interprets his passion and death in the words of his prayer: "I have made known thy name to the men whom thou didst give me out of the world" (John 17:6); again, he says, "The world must be shown that I love the Father and do exactly as he commands; so up, let us go forward" (John 14:31). As the members of the Church act and suffer in the same spirit as Jesus—with the same love for the Father and for the redeemed—so Jesus, through them, continues his redemption: "I have sent them into the world...that the world may believe that thou didst send me" (John 17:19, 21).

Prayer

O divine and human heart of my Savior, if I did not know and love you, the sufferings of humankind and my own sufferings would crush me. But turning my eyes to you, I can only praise you for having freed me from senseless suffering and from a hopeless death.

It is not you, our beloved Redeemer, who has brought suffering into this world. It is due to humanity's sinfulness. But, in your unlimited love, you decided to plunge into the ocean of our suffering to baptize and to transfigure it by your own blood.

If, in faith and trust, we accept our share of suffering for the salvation of humankind in union with your death and resurrection, then we are no longer slaves of suffering and the fear of death. Because of our fidelity to you, suffering no longer alienates us from each other; we are no longer oppressed by feelings of guilt. Rather, suffering becomes a salvific approach to a greater love of your heart and a liberating love for our neighbor.

Lord, increase my faith, my trust in you, my love, so that I can say "yes" to suffering and death, praising you for the meaning and redemptive power you give to them. And so I beg you to grant me—through the power of your Spirit—the strength to praise you unceasingly in the midst of suffering. I thank you for having united me and my suffering with your mission as Redeemer of the world.

Amen.

13

Personal Consecration to the Sacred Heart

I pray thee, not to take them out of the world, but to keep them from the Evil One. They are strangers in the world, as I am. Consecrate them by the truth; thy word is truth. As thou hast sent me into the world, I have sent them into the world, and for their sake, I now consecrate myself, that they too may be consecrated by the truth.

JOHN 17:15–19

PERSONAL CONSECRATION TO THE SACRED HEART

From the very moment of the Incarnation of the Word of God, the humanity of Jesus Christ is consecrated to the glory of the Father and the salvation of humankind. The conscious life of Jesus is a constant "yes" to this mission and consecration. The high-priestly prayer offered to the Father in the presence of his chosen witnesses on the eve of his passion and death—the eve on which he gave us the perpetual memorial of his death and resurrection—is his solemn consecration, the perfect expression of his loving dedication. And we, his disciples, are inserted into this consecration prayer.

Jesus accepts us gratefully as gift of the Father. He loves us—despite our striking drawbacks—as belonging to the Father. He makes us his friends and even a part of his love for the Father, and he consecrates us to be sharers in his own mission to the glory of the Father and redemption of the world.

This, however, implies that, through Jesus and in him, we, his disciples, are made one. He prays, "Holy Father, protect by the power of thy name those whom thou hast given me, that they may be one, as we are one" (John 17:11). He continues, "I speak these words, so that they may have my joy within them in full measure" (John 17:13). He, the Messiah—in the words of the psalmist—is anointed with the oil of gladness. "My joy" is a sign of his consecration and readiness for fulfillment of his mission. The "gladness" makes him the "Good News" in person. Hence, his disciples' participation in his mission implies their sharing in his joy, in the overflow of his love for the Father, and in the fulfillment of his mission.

"Consecrate them by the truth, thy word is truth." The Word sent to us by the Father and the word Jesus speaks to us by his whole life are the truth that breathes love and bears fruit in love, joy, and peace. That our hearts and minds should be filled by this truth is an essential part of our election and dedication to share in Jesus' mission in the world. Jesus solemnly consecrates us to this with the prayer: "And for their sake, I now consecrate myself, that they too may be consecrated by the truth."

The consecration to the Sacred Heart of Jesus, which is a substantial component of this devotion, should be thoroughly understood in the light of Jesus' own consecration prayer, which stayed with him, in his heart, mind, and will, unto his last breath and his last heartbeat on the cross.

This prayer should be particularly dear to priests who, in a special way, are consecrated for the ministry of the word and the sacraments in configuration with Christ. But the Church rightly desires that all the faithful should consecrate themselves to the heart of Jesus and thus to the heavenly Father. Each one should open his or her heart and will to Jesus' own prayer of consecration, in which all are included.

Baptism, as sacrament of faith and faithfulness, is already in itself a real and permanent consecration to the triune God; it establishes an intimate relationship to Christ and his cause. The sacrament of confirmation is meant to bring this to completion through the anointment consecration by the Holy Spirit; it shows us clearly the road to a life consecrated for the kingdom of God. But all this needs to enter ever more into our conscious life of commitment.

The grace of God, freely granted, calls for a free and conscious response. This consecration must enter fully into our fundamental option and inform all levels of our conscious life. As we do this, we should remember that the concept of "heart" denotes the all-embracing, all-informing depth—the vital center of our total response to God. And how could our "heart" become more alive than by being conformed to the heart of Jesus, with his infinite love for the Father and for us?

Consecration to the heart of Jesus is, above all, a believing prayer that our hearts, minds, wills, memories, and discernments may be formed by the love of Jesus, for which his open heart, the heart of the risen Christ, stands as cherished symbol. We consecrate ourselves to the service of his love, so that many will come to know lovingly the design of Jesus and the Father. In consecrating ourselves, we enter into Christ's own prayer of consecration and do so with great trust in the transforming power of his Spirit.

This is a profound self-commitment to strive at all times and under all circumstances toward a holy life of redeemed and redeeming love as a response to God's gracious action and appeal. It is our firm "yes" to the sanctifying and consecrating action of God and to our vocation to a saving solidarity of the redeemed. It is a sign of our zeal for the salvation of all as we constantly battle against the solidarity of perdition.

The prayer of consecration to the Sacred Heart can and should bear personal traits, since it is expected to rise from within our own hearts. Furthermore, we should note that its contents will change as our life situations change. We offer here some models so that everyone will realize how the prayer may differ from time to time.

Consecration Prayer of an Unknown Author at Trier in the Fifteenth Century

O golden gate, opened by the spear of Longinus, heart of the Savior, here I enter into my safe refuge, the secure place of my beatitude.

To your opened heart, O Jesus, I offer, I entrust, I consecrate my heart, my soul, my body, my life, and my death, all joys and sufferings of mine. Everything is yours and no longer mine, everything is yours entirely forever and for all eternity.

When my heart shall break in the hour of death, O living, wounded heart, receive me and enclose me wholly in your heart. May your wounded heart be the first thing I look upon and become my first repose.

Amen.

Consecration Prayer
of Saint Margaret Mary Alacoque

Most holy heart of Jesus, fullness of love, be my protection in life and pledge of eternal salvation. Be my strength in weakness and inconsistency. Be atonement for all sins of my life.

O heart, gentle and kind, be our refuge in the hour of our death. Be our justification before God. Turn away from us the punishment of your just wrath.

O loving heart, in you we put all our trust. From our weakness, we have to fear everything; from your love, we hope everything. Blot out what could displease you; impress your love so deeply on our heart that we never again forget you, that we never can be separated from you.

Lord and Savior, for the sake of your love, we plead that our name be imprinted in your most holy heart. Let it be our happiness and honor to serve you in life and death.

Consecration Prayer of Denis the Carthusian

O Lord Jesus Christ, in union with the praise by which you honor God in all eternity, I desire to offer you this praise and these prayers. I implore your boundless mercy to grant me a contrite and devoted heart; a humble, chaste, and zealous heart; a faithful and pure heart; a heart according to your heart, sanctified in your heart, drawn to your heart; a heart totally open to receive you: that I may not be attached to anything besides you, that I may not look for anything and not seek anything except you, that I may praise and thank you always, loving you always in all things and above all things.

Amen.

Consecration Prayer of St. John Henry Newman

O Heart of Jesus, all Love, I offer thee these humble prayers for myself and for all those who unite themselves with me in spirit to adore thee. O holiest Heart of Jesus most lovely, I intend to renew and to offer to thee these acts of adoration and these prayers for me, a wretched sinner, and for all those who are associated in thy adoration. Help me to do this throughout my entire life, even unto its end.

I recommend to thee, O my Jesus, the holy Church, thy dear spouse, and our true mother, the souls who practice justice, all poor sinners, the afflicted, the dying, and all humankind. Let not thy blood be shed for them in vain.

Finally, deign to apply it in relief of the souls in purgatory, those in particular who have practiced in the course of their life this holy devotion of adoring thee.

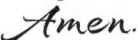

Consecration Prayer of Pope Pius XI

Most beloved Jesus, Savior of humankind, look mercifully upon us who kneel in humility before your altar. Yours we are and yours we want to remain. That we might belong more intimately to you, each and all of us consecrate ourselves to your most holy heart.

Many have never come to know you, many have despised your commandments and have turned away from you. Kindest Jesus, have pity upon them and draw them all to your most holy heart. Lord, king not only of the faithful who have never abandoned you but also of your children who have gone astray, grant that soon they may return to the Father's house, so that they may not perish in misery and starvation.

Manifest yourself as king also of those who are deceived by error or severed by schism. Call them back to the safe home of truth and unity of faith, so that there will be one sheepfold and one shepherd.

Show yourself as king of all who live imprisoned in the darkness of paganism or in Islam. Lead them into the light of your reign.

Look mercifully upon the children of the people that you first have chosen. May your blood flow upon them as fountain of redemption and life.

Lord, grant your Church welfare, security, and freedom. Grant all nations peace and order. Grant that, from one end of the earth to the other, the shout may resound: "Praise be to the divine heart through which salvation has come; praise and glory to him in all eternity."

Consecration Prayer of Religious Men and Women

Kindest Lord and Master, when before your passion, you solemnly consecrated yourself for the salvation of the world, you graciously included me in that consecration. The blessing of that consecration has abundantly reached my heart in holy baptism, in confirmation, and in the holy Eucharist as a stream of grace by which you have introduced me into the riches of your loving heart and united me with your body and your blood shed for me.

I thank you that, time and again, you have touched my heart by your grace and called me to intimate friendship. I thank you for all the graces you have lavished upon me at the altar when I offered you my religious vows. I thank you for accepting my offering despite my weakness and for consecrating me by your love and accompanying me lovingly along the way.

I now renew my consecration to confirm and deepen my baptismal and religious vows, with deep sorrow that so many times I did not fulfill them with unbroken fidelity; still, I consecrate myself now with great trust in your forgiving and healing love.

Lord, accept me as I am and make me what you want me to be. Take away from me everything that stands in the way of your love and grant me everything that leads me to fullest union with you. I thank you, most loving Master, for having called me to be a witness to your love for all, and I thank you particularly for enabling me to love and serve those who are poor and unloved, so that they may feel a ray of your own love.

In this renewed consecration, I pray especially for my community. Make us one in your heart, so that together we can help the world find you, the Savior of all.

O Mary, Mother of our Redeemer and our Mother, you are nearest to the heart of your Son. In each moment of your life, you confirmed your "yes" to your great vocation. Pray for me that my further life will hold to this consecration.

14

WORLD CONSECRATION TO THE SACRED HEART

Thou art merciful to all men because thou canst do all things; thou dost overlook the sins of men to bring them to repentance, for all existing things are dear to thee and thou hatest nothing that thou hast created—why else wouldst thou have made it? How could anything have continued in existence, had it not been thy will?...Thou sparest all things because they are thine, our Lord and Master who lovest all that lives, for thy imperishable breath is in them all.

For this reason, thou dost correct offenders little by little, admonishing them and reminding them of their sins, in order that they may leave their evil ways and put their trust in you, O Lord, in thee.

WISDOM OF SOLOMON, 11:23—12:2

God cannot but love everything he has created. Yet we are astonished that he loves a world so entangled in sin. We are amazed to see his mercy extended to a world that has rebelled against its Creator, has afflicted itself with terrible misery.

As we look at Jesus, the Redeemer of the world, we are even more astonished than the author of the Book of Wisdom. Forever Jesus heartily loves the world for whose redemption the Father sent him and for which he has shed his heart's blood. In his consecration prayer (John 17), Jesus shares his own consecration with his disciples, whom he is sending into the world to make known to all people the love with which he, the Redeemer, loves the world. The disciples are called to be holy, to be one in heart and mind, so that the world may receive a taste of the love with which the Father sent his only Son to redeem it.

In his high-priestly prayer, Jesus gives two quite different connotations to the word "world." This becomes evident in the text and through the context. There is the "godless world," the leading class of Jerusalem, the religious and political leaders of that moment, who obstinately reject the call to salvation and to grateful love because of their individual and collective egotism and lust for power. The disciples must be aware of that godless world, of the temptations that arise from it, and its persecution against those who proclaim the Gospel in its fullness and truth.

And there is the other "world" about which Jesus speaks. It is redeemed by him, and he is ready to die—even though it is a world in which good and bad are appallingly interwoven. This world will always be in need of God's mercy. It will need convincing testimony not just from one individual disciple of Jesus but also from the community of disciples who, by their oneness in heart and mind, reflect the divine love and saving purpose of Christ.

The traditional devotion to the Sacred Heart received an important clarification and broadening of horizons through Pope Leo XIII who, in his encyclical *Annum Sacrum* (1899), called for the consecration of the whole world to the Sacred Heart. In this document, certain privatizing tendencies are clearly rejected. Jesus wants to draw to himself all human hearts so that they may join him in his all-inclusive love as sharers of his mission to be Redeemer and Liberator of humanity. Jesus wants more than the love of a heart that concerns itself only with its own spirituality. The Church knows that it is chosen, sent, and conquered by the heart of Jesus for the salvation of the world.

The consecration of the whole world to the Sacred Heart also unmasks mistaken activists who think they can liberate the world by their own power, by manipulation of the world's cultural, economic, and sociopolitical structures. These manipulators corrupt themselves and all fundamental human relationships. Because their trust is only in themselves and their manipulative skills, they easily tend to violence, class hatred, and war—ideology against ideology, nation against nation.

Even if someone were to discover an exemplary political constitution, the best form of economic life, and the ideal structures of culture, and if such a person had the skill and power to manipulate humanity to accept this overall plan, the world would not become any better. In the hands of manipulated manipulators, everything would turn out wrong.

The most urgent and, indeed, the only effective remedy for healing the public life is a change of heart that would liberate us from individual and collective egotism by conversion to true love and justice. In the final analysis, this means the turning of hearts to the fountain of love that is opened to us in the heart of Jesus.

Even in Old Testament times, there were prophets, especially Jeremiah and Ezekiel, who spoke of the "heart renewed" and a "new covenant" as coordinated realities. Together, they were to form a new saving solidarity among men and women, first in view of the "sacred remnant" but eventually in respect to all peoples. This "sacred remnant" is composed of those who, "one in heart and mind," turn to the Redeemer of the world.

The consecration of the world to the Sacred Heart, through individual communities and the whole Church, is a solemn act of commitment to redemptive solidarity, a commitment to the mission received from the divine Master to be "salt for the earth" and "light for the world."

No one can join in this consecration without a readiness to shoulder his or her part of co-responsibility for the salvation of the world.

A genuine dynamic of truth exists in this co-responsibility for the welfare and salvation of the whole of humanity in view of the Sacred Heart of the Redeemer of the world. What the world needs more than anything else are loving hearts and healthy human relationships—people who radiate peace and love, who build bridges between heart and heart, enkindling light and warmth and leading to an all-inclusive holistic vision. The basic symbol of this wholeness and solidarity is "the heart of humanity."

Since the time of Pope Leo XIII, our Catholic social doctrine has insisted on the inseparability of change of heart and change of social conditions. We must commit ourselves to both dimensions but change of heart receives top priority. Change of heart is the healthy and indispensable source of all effective efforts to transform the economic, cultural, social, and political conditions of the world for the better. There is no way to bring about a healthy economic world order without sincere intentions and motives by all who are willing to work for it. Surely, we need structural remedies too, but they fulfill their purpose only when the hearts of people meet in sincere dedication to healing justice.

Those who unite with their local and universal Church and consecrate themselves to the Sacred Heart must be aware of the ambiguity of the "world" and of their own hearts. Both are in need of redemption. Only with great trust in the Redeemer of the world can we fight against this dual ambiguity. Our consecration will therefore involve us in persistent prayer for the healing of our own hearts—of all human relationships—and commitment to the healing of public life.

Those who authentically venerate the Sacred Heart never think just of self-fulfillment or only of saving their own souls. They are consecrated to the salvation of the whole world. This weakens in no way their striving for personal wholeness and holiness; rather, it strengthens them in the total context of a saving solidarity. We pray then for them: "For all of humankind, I consecrate myself, that they too may be consecrated, truly redeemed."

Consecration of the world, as a solemn commitment to the salvation of the world by believing communities, does not tolerate shallow optimism and even less a dangerous pessimism that weakens all our inner resources. The heart of Jesus, pierced and opened, contradicts the pessimist's conclusion that the world is a hopeless case and that flight from it would be the better course. Those who truly venerate the heart of Jesus do not abandon ship or give up hope. The purpose of our effort to gain a healthy distance from the temptations of the world is to become a purified, sincere, healthy, and healing presence in the world. The healing of public life needs this kind of honesty in the fullest sense: absolute sincerity and generosity.

Prayer

O my Redeemer, Savior of the world, the more I am touched by a ray of your love, the more I experience liberation from narrowness and cowardliness. In your divine and human heart, there is room for the whole world. I realize now how impossible it is to love you without joining you in your all-inclusive love.

This gives a new meaning to my commitment to your heart. It becomes ever more a "yes" to your consecrating prayer at the Last Supper. I thank you for thus consecrating yourself for the salvation of the world and for including us, your disciples, in this consecration. I thank you for sending us out into the world with the same love and the same mandate of love and peace with which your heavenly Father sent you into this world.

I praise you for letting your light shine upon us so much that, in your light, we poor creatures can become "light for the world." Drawn irresistibly by your consecration to the salvation of the world, I renounce all selfishness of heart. O Lord, free me from all self-seeking interests. I want to do everything that will help people to open their hearts to one another in mutual respect, justice, and compassion. I long for a heart full of compassion for the suffering and full of dedication to the poor and unloved. My purpose is not to write off the rich and powerful of this world; I want only to bring to them and to all who enjoy influence in public life the saving message that they too are redeemed and can join in effective actions for the healing of public life. Help me to convince them that they are not irrevocably condemned to be enslaved by the voracious gods of riches and power. I want to cry from the rooftops to the hearts of all people that they can be freed for the work of justice and peace by redeeming love.

O Sacred Heart of my Redeemer and Savior of the world, I would never make bold to join the Church in the consecration of the whole of humanity if I dared not put all my trust in you. Cleanse, broaden, and strengthen our hearts so that we may truly become what you want us to be: light for the world.

Amen.

15

Family Consecration to the Sacred Heart

Let the Holy Spirit fill you: speak to one another in psalms, hymns, and songs; sing and make music in your hearts to the Lord; and in the name of our Lord Jesus Christ, give thanks every day for everything to our God and Father.

Be subject to one another out of reverence for Christ.…Husbands, love your wives, as Christ also loved the Church and gave himself up for it, to consecrate it, cleansing it by water and word, so that he might present the Church to himself all glorious, with no stain or wrinkle or anything of the sort, but holy and without blemish. In the same way, men also are bound to love their wives as they love their own bodies.

EPHESIANS 5:18–21, 25–28

FAMILY CONSECRATION TO THE SACRED HEART

The family is a most privileged place where heart meets heart and heart speaks to heart. Therefore, it is in accord with the "logic of the heart" that Christian families consecrate themselves to the heart of Jesus. Husbands and wives, parents and children, brothers and sisters can love each other as redeemed people with a love whose wellspring is the heart of Jesus. Loving familial relationships and authentic veneration of the Sacred Heart need each other and foster each other.

A Christian family that consecrates itself entirely to the Sacred Heart resolves to participate in Jesus' self-consecration. It was obviously Christ's intention that the families of his disciples might be "truly consecrated." It is not too difficult to discern the essential traits. In his consecration prayer, Jesus sees his disciples as a precious gift of the heavenly Father to him, and he, on his part, makes of himself a total gift to his disciples, even to death on a cross. In each Eucharistic celebration, we relive this mutuality: Jesus accepts us as gift of the Father and makes a gift of himself to us, and we are enabled by his Spirit to entrust ourselves as a grateful gift to him. Thus, our consecration is confirmed and deepened.

Marital love reaches its sublime nobility in the basic relationship of husband and wife. God has given them mutual love, and he has given each one to the other as his gift; in their mutual love, he, the giver of all good gifts, is lovingly present. In the measure that spouses love one another, each one sees the other as a wonderful gift.

In view of this, the Second Vatican Council does not speak of marriage as a "contract" but as a "covenant in mutual self-bestowal." It is a covenant of mutual love inserted into the new and everlasting covenant between Christ and his Church.

Good parents honor their children as gifts of God and as the crowning of their mutual love. Parents transmit life in its fully human value only when they welcome their children as sharers in the mutuality of their love or, we might say, as concelebrants of the everlasting covenant of love. Happy the children who feel each day that their parents—by their actions and by their words—are saying to them, "It is good that you are; it is wonderful that God has given you to us; it is a joy for us to live for each other!" If this experience is radically present, then it will be quite natural that brothers and sisters will also accept and affirm each other as gifts that have more value than all material things.

The Christian family that takes its bearings from the heart of Jesus is a most valuable school for learning redeemed and redeeming love for each other and likewise for others. The mutual respect of its members for each other and their deference to each other for the sake of the common good have their model in the loving obedience of Jesus to his heavenly Father; in his loving dedication to his "new family," the redeemed; and in the grateful love of the Church for its Savior.

The spirit of a good Christian family is marked by praise and thanksgiving. Family prayer in praise of God and of our Lord Jesus Christ confirms and deepens the mutual bonds of loving reverence. It helps members of the family to discover in each other the rich inner resources for shared growth in whatever is good, beautiful, and true, and it gives them mutual encouragement in their struggles against dangerous attachments.

From shared praise and thanksgiving comes the vital insight that God accepts each member of this family as he or she is. He takes each one by the hand to guide him or her, according to his design, on the way to maturity, when the full stature of Christ will become visible in them. Thus, they grow in redeemed co-humanity for each other and for all of God's household.

In this spirit of faith and adoration, the members of the family ever more consciously become companions for each other on the road to wholeness and holiness. They learn together from Jesus the great commandment: "Love one another as I have loved you" (John 15:12). They learn to bear each other's burdens, as Paul indicates in Galatians 6:2.

In faithful service to them, the stronger ones will help the weaker ones. In a healthy family, its members have patience with each other. And when one member of the family develops problems, he or she will be helped not only by kind correction but even more by loving trust—just as Jesus acts with us.

If an entire family consecrates itself to the Sacred Heart, as several popes have recommended, this can greatly contribute to a clear and purposeful orientation for mutual love and creative co-responsibility. But this also implies a firm orientation of the family to participate in the work of redemption, of healing people, and of healing public life. And, to do this, they must radiate kindness, goodness, generosity, and co-responsibility in their environment among friends and neighbors.

Prayer

Beloved Savior, we thank you with all our hearts. By your life in the Holy Family of Nazareth, you have consecrated the Christian family and have made it a privileged school of holiness in mutual love. Coming from the heart of the Father, you chose to learn humble love by living in the bosom of a human family. Your whole life is marked by the love you have received from your Mother and from St. Joseph, her gracious spouse. You were glad to love them in return and thus to enrich your beloved ones. We cannot think of your heart's love for people and of your compassionate teaching without being reminded of the family wherein all this unfolded as you grew in age and wisdom.

We thank you also for the mutual love of our parents, which was the fountainhead of their love for us.

We thank you for the love and affirmation received from our brothers and sisters, echoing the love of our parents. May this wealth of love bear fruit in all our relationships, and may it give us the strength to love unloved people.

Most loving heart of Jesus, when you consecrated yourself to the Father for our salvation, you prayed that we, too, might be consecrated in truth. So, we consecrate our family to you and, with you, to the Father. Consecrated to your loving heart, we intend to help each other faithfully grow in love for you and for each other.

Consecrated to your heart, we shall safeguard the sincerity and fidelity of our love. We will help each other discover the inner resources in each of us and all of us for growth in love and responsibility. Teach us as a family to reach out to others, to accept and grant friendship, and to associate ourselves with others in our striving for the welfare and salvation of all.

Lord, accept our consecration, accept our mutual love. Cleanse and strengthen it, and make it a source of blessing for many.

Amen.

16

STREAMS OF LIVING WATER

On the last and greatest day of the festival, Jesus stood and cried aloud, "If anyone is thirsty, let him come to me; whoever believes in me, let him drink." As Scripture says, "Streams of living water shall flow out from within him." He was speaking of the Spirit, which believers in him would receive later; for the Spirit had not yet been given, because Jesus had not yet been glorified.

JOHN 7:37–39

One of the soldiers stabbed his side with a lance, and at once there was a flow of blood and water. This is vouched for by an eyewitness, whose evidence is to be trusted.

JOHN 19:34–35

STREAMS OF LIVING WATER

The symbol of "streams of living water," which first must flow from the pierced heart of the Redeemer before they can flow from the believers, is a well-known heritage of our devotion to the Sacred Heart. It is one of its biblical foundations that attracted many hearts. With the opening of the heart of the Redeemer, who with his last breath has entrusted his Spirit to the Father, the first act of glorification of the Father is accomplished. It will be followed by the glorification of the Son, through the Father, in Christ's resurrection and in the outpouring of the Holy Spirit.

From the fountain of salvation, we drink the great gift of redemption, the Holy Spirit, who opens our hearts for redeemed love and fills them from the overflow of boundless love emerging out of the heart of Jesus. "God's love has flooded our inmost heart through the Holy Spirit he has given us" (Romans 5:5). Urgently, Jesus invites us to drink from this fountain, not just enough to quench our own thirst, but enough to strengthen us to become for others a fountain of saving love.

For his great encyclical on the Sacred Heart, Pope Pius XII chose as opening words, "Haurietis aquas," from the text of the prophet: "And so you shall draw water with joy from the springs of deliverance" (Isaiah 12:3). This is cause for rejoicing, thanksgiving, and praise: "Cry out, shout aloud, you that dwell in Zion, for the Holy One of Israel is among you in majesty" (Isaiah 12:6). The image reminds us of Moses, whom God told to summon living water from a rock. And Paul says, "They all drank from the supernatural rock that accompanied their travels—and that rock was Christ" (1 Corinthians 10:4).

In his encyclical, Pope Pius XII says, "This intimate bond between divine love, which should inflame the hearts of believers, and the Holy Spirit, as indicated by Scripture, splendidly characterizes the real nature of the devotion that is offered to the most sacred heart of Jesus."

The first thing for us to do, therefore, is to quench our thirst for redeeming love at the fountain of deliverance, as Jesus invited us to do: "If anyone is thirsty, let him come to me!" The Holy Spirit, through the ministry of salvation in the Church, continues to invite us, and everyone who has tasted the streams of living water will eagerly pass on to others this same invitation: "'Come!' say the Spirit and the bride. 'Come!' let each hearer reply. Come forward, you who are thirsty, accept the water of life, a free gift to all who desire it" (Revelation 22:17).

Jesus himself, who on the cross was both humiliated and exalted, extends to us his abundant love, the source of life. "The lamb who is at the heart of the throne will be their shepherd and will guide them to the springs of the water of life" (Revelation 7:17).

The Holy Spirit, the third person in the Holy Trinity, is the personified gift by which the Father eternally gives himself to the Word, his Son, and the Word returns his love and himself as gift to the Father. In his humanity, Jesus is anointed and sent by the Spirit for the work of redemption. In the power of the same Spirit, Jesus offers himself on the cross as a sacrificial gift to the Father for our sake. And with the flow of blood and water from his opened heart, he becomes the fountain of the gift of the Holy Spirit for us.

By the same power of the Spirit through which Jesus has made himself a sin-offering for us sinners, he gives himself in the Eucharist as a source of everlasting love for us. And the glorious circle becomes perfect in that Jesus sends us the Holy Spirit from the Father to enable us to give our hearts to and entrust ourselves to the Father in union with Jesus. Thus, all our lives become an expression of grateful love and of lasting praise for such an undeserved gift.

This "superabundant redemption" manifests itself particularly when those who have appeased their thirst at the fountain of the water of life and are captured by the love of Jesus become one with Christ, so that "streams of living water" flow out from within them.

The definite biblical teaching is that no one can have a vital share in the love of the Redeemer without joining him actively in his love for all. The gift of the Spirit cannot be buried in a selfish heart. Through unceasing thanksgiving for these gifts, our hearts will become more and more fashioned after the heart of Jesus, Redeemer of the world. As a consequence, during our entire lives, we shall urge all who are thirsty to come to Jesus and to drink from his love.

The consecration of ourselves and of the world to the heart of Jesus must be seen in this light. If we are consecrated by the Holy Spirit to the love of the Redeemer of the world, we consciously accept our mission: "As thou hast sent me into the world, I have sent them into the world, and for their sake, I now consecrate myself" (John 17:18–19). Jesus makes it clear that this mission and this consecration come to us as a transforming, renewing power of the Spirit: "Jesus repeated, 'Peace be with you!' and said, 'As the Father sent me, so I send you.' Then he breathed on them, saying, 'Receive the Holy Spirit!'" (John 20:20–22).

What we and the whole world most urgently need is the love that flows from the heart of Jesus, pierced for us and glorified by the Father. The beginning of the way of salvation is to have a great thirst for this love, without which we cannot be salt for the earth and light for the world. If we are alert to how much the world needs this greatest of all gifts, this awareness will increase our own desires and endeavors. It is this that matters for all of us.

Prayer

Most loving Lord and Master, the terrible thirst that you suffered when you were losing the last drops of your precious blood is a heartbreaking symbol of your thirst to share with us the riches of your love and your redemption. We thank you for constantly inviting us—through your own voice from the cross, through the voice of the "Spirit and the bride," and through the voices of all venerators of your heart—to drink thirstily at the fountain of salvation so that the water of life can flow from within us to others.

Send forth your Spirit to awaken in us this thirst. Let your thirst become ours; let your love become our love for all the redeemed, so that all may come to experience this love and become ever thirstier for a greater love.

We know that we can pray with complete trust if we look at what your heart desires most for us. So, we come to pray not for small things but for the greatest of all gifts: that you draw us so much to your heart that we long to see all people drawn to this same love. Then there will be goodness and peace throughout the world, and you can hand us all over to the Father as your gift.

Lord Jesus, the blood and water that flowed from your pierced heart on the cross represented streams of salvation for all. We beg you, send us your Holy Spirit to renew our hearts, to cleanse them and inflame them with your love: love for you, love for our brothers and sisters all over the world. Grant us a joyful, grateful, and strong faith, for only from within true believers can the streams of the water of life flow to others.

Amen.

17

Heart of Jesus and God's People

Christ also loved the Church and gave himself up for it, to consecrate it, cleansing it by water and word, so that he might present the Church to himself all glorious, with no stain or wrinkle or anything of the sort, but holy and without blemish.

Ephesians 5:25–27

HEART OF JESUS AND GOD'S PEOPLE

The Old Testament shows that God's adoption of a nation is ordered to the people as a whole. Individuals were regarded more in the light of members of a people. God is the "spouse," the "good shepherd" of his people. In the New Testament, these images correspond to the relationship of Christ to his Church. The Twelve Apostles, the cornerstones of the Church, point to a continuity with the once-united twelve tribes of the chosen people.

The covenant sealed by the blood of the Redeemer, which we celebrate in the Eucharist as God's people, is the covenant of love with the Church, but, unlike the former, in this covenant, each member is held in his or her own uniqueness. Of course, the Church points collectively to all of humankind.

Since the time of the Fathers of the Church, theology has held that the Church is born from the opened heart of Jesus. His heart's blood is the Church's dowry. To the Church, the streams of salvation flow as gift of the Spirit. Jesus, in his overwhelming and faithful love, has chosen the Church, not because of merit on its side, but only out of his own gratuitous love. He has given the Church life by his redemption, has called it into being by his creative word, and has bestowed on it the promise to abide with it until the end of time.

The Church can understand itself, its worth, and its mission only as coming from the love of Jesus Christ. Hence, its first and fundamental task is to learn to know and to love

Jesus. In this way, the Church learns to love all people in union with Jesus' own love. The Church is the sacrament of salvation insofar as it makes visible—through its members, its charisms, its ministries, its structure, its liturgy, and even its laws and their application—the love of Jesus and its love for him in return. The Church is called to radiate that love, which should flow from it as a stream of living water.

For this purpose, an authentic devotion to the Sacred Heart is most fitting and fruitful. It is a tremendous challenge to the Church and its self-understanding because, in this devotion of devotions, what matters above all is to be touched and moved by the love of the Sacred Heart and to love, with Jesus, the heavenly Father and all the redeemed. This devotion also prompts an ongoing examination of conscience, which looks at the conduct of the entire Church and the lives of each of its members. The result is often a deep sorrow or even a profound shock that we, as members, and the Church have responded so poorly to the love that has chosen us and continues to give us life. Our reaction should lead us to humble confession and, at the same time, to grateful praise of his enduring mercy despite our want of fidelity. But, of course, this praise makes sense only when we renew our purpose to respond to this divine fidelity through a much more steadfast faithfulness. We should be no longer a source of disappointment for Jesus.

The Church is meant to be a source of joy for its divine spouse. Jesus rejoices that the Father has entrusted the

Church to him as his gift. He exults over those who humbly and gratefully respond to his love. He recognizes not only the saints canonized by the Church but also all the hidden saints and the many who, despite enormous obstacles, strive for total conversion. He looks with kindness upon the poor sinners who have learned to put all their trust in him. There is great rejoicing in heaven over each of them.

Jesus looks with heartfelt delight on the preaching of conversion through the Church if it is coupled with the Church's readiness for ongoing renewal of all aspects of its life. The heart of Jesus welcomes the new thrust in many parts of Christianity toward reunion of our separated brothers and sisters, especially if these efforts are marked by great humility.

But the Church has also cost the heart of Jesus many pains. Because he so deeply loved his disciples, the suffering Messiah was often saddened by their stubbornness and rivalry, their resistance to his real mission. Time and again, when he explained his mission to free humankind from pride and arrogance by humble service, his disciples began disputing about which of them would play the most important role in his kingdom. Even when Jesus had washed their feet and explained what this was meant to teach them, they refused to accept it. These and many other incidents must have given Jesus a frightening picture of all the troubles his Church would endure from people calling themselves "Christians."

The extreme suffering of Jesus' heart and soul on the eve of his passion was increased by the apathy and sleepiness of his beloved disciples, from whom he should have been able to expect sympathy and consolation. But these are not just past events. They are repeated also in our time, even by ourselves, who give so little thought to being a source of joy for all, to the glory of Jesus Christ.

If we look at the heart of Jesus or if we see his eyes turned to us, we shall not be tempted to sit in judgment on the "Church," forgetting that we are a part of it and a partial cause of its imperfection and its distress. It is you and I, members of the Church, who harm it by our sin and negligence. We hide the Church's true identity from people.

It is true that a deep knowledge and love of Jesus call for self-criticism of all members of the Church, including its leaders. We should suffer with Jesus when we see partial failures in the Church, failures of the Church's mission caused by lack of holiness. But if it is really the love of Jesus that seizes and stimulates us, we shall always begin with criticism of ourselves. And our critical awareness of the imperfections of structures and leaders in the Church should merge with Christ's mercy and compassion and increase our own striving for holiness.

When we look at the Church in view of Jesus, we shall be ever more gratefully aware of all the good we have received and still receive in the Church and from the Church. If we realize how difficult it is for institutional traditions of the

Church to change and to enter fully into Jesus' mandate for unity in diversity, we shall praise the Lord even more that so much healthy reform has been possible. Especially, we shall praise him for the saints who teach us by their lives that individual conversion and fruitful commitment for Church renewal are possible if we put our trust in the Lord.

Our relationship with the Church as its members is healthy if we consider everything in the light of the love of Jesus for his Church. We see the Church arising from his pierced heart, flowing from it with the blood and water released by the lance. Thus, it is clear that we cannot drink from the water of salvation if we bypass the Church, its ministry of the word, and its sacraments.

Our wounded relationships with the real Church will be healed if we look at the Church in this light. Saint Augustine writes about the Church as opening the gateway to life for him. He says that through it flow the sacraments of the Church and that nothing has more power to heal than this wound. "Through this gate comes salvation, through it we enter into the reign of love."

Prayer

All-loving Savior, we praise you for the great love you have bestowed on your Church—despite its shortcomings. You have accepted the Church as a gift created by the heavenly Father. You have shed the last drop of your heart's blood for the Church. It has an abiding abode in your heart.

I want to unite myself with all the grateful love that you have received from your Church, from its saints and penitents. With the entire Church, I praise you for your boundless faithfulness and the healing powers flowing from your heart to cure our lack of faithfulness. I unite my sorrow and penitence with all the saintly penitents of the past and present, and with all who venerate your Sacred Heart, especially those who have offered you atonement in union with the atonement that you have offered for us to your Father.

I want to join you in your great and steadfast love for your Church and to learn from you how to love it with the same kind of everlasting love you have for it. Help me by your grace gratefully to accept my place in the Church and to serve it faithfully and sincerely.

Assist your Church in growing in the knowledge and love of your Sacred Heart. Bless your Church so that it may be able to lead many people to love you.

Amen.

18

Eucharistic Heart of Jesus

Jesus answered, "I tell you this: the truth is, not that Moses gave you the bread from heaven, but that my Father gives you the real bread from heaven. The bread that God gives comes down from heaven and brings life to the world." They said to him, "Sir, give us this bread now and always." Jesus said to them, "I am the bread of life. Whoever comes to me shall never be hungry, and whoever believes in me shall never be thirsty."

JOHN 6:32–35

EUCHARISTIC HEART OF JESUS

History shows that devotion to the Sacred Heart of Jesus and a great love for the Eucharist are inseparable. This is most evident in the lives of St. Gertrude and St. Mechtilde. Their devotion to the Sacred Heart was centered in the liturgy. The celebration of the Eucharist inspired them to contemplate and to praise the loving heart of Jesus, who, seated at the right hand of the Father, constantly intercedes for us. Jesus, who gave us this memorial of his sacrificial and atoning love, is now present in the Eucharist to bestow on us the wonderful pledge of the love of his heart. It is especially in the Eucharist that he offers us, as it were, an "exchange of heart," conforming our hearts to his heart.

The adoration of Jesus in the Eucharist and union with him in praise of the Father are at the very center of St. John Eudes' devotion to the Sacred Heart. His zeal to have the mystery of Jesus' heart honored by a special feast and liturgy—which, in turn, compelled him to emphasize the atoning love for Jesus in this great sacrament of the Eucharist—deserves our grateful love.

Only with deep sorrow can we think of how many people remain ungrateful and even directly dishonor the Lord in the Eucharist. Saint John Eudes summons us to special atonement for all the sins against the loving eucharistic heart of Jesus. This atonement, centered in a grateful and sacrificial love, stands ready to offer everything that love demands in reparation for the sins of ingratitude. And St.

John Eudes is well aware that our atonement can have value only in union with the sacrifice of Christ, a union of heart and mind to which Jesus invites us and makes possible for us in the Eucharist.

The spirituality of St. Margaret Mary Alacoque exhibits a similar emphasis. She was convinced that souls totally captured by the eucharistic love of Jesus can be a source of atonement and, by their adoring and generous love, can somehow provide a balance for the terrible coldness and hardness of so many hearts. This saint also promoted the liturgical celebration of the mystery of the Sacred Heart with the same zeal as St. John Eudes.

It should be noted here that these classical promoters of the devotion to the Sacred Heart show no privatizing tendency. On the contrary, they express salvation-solidarity. We should also remember that St. John Eudes and St. Margaret Mary Alacoque greatly helped to overcome Jansenism, which, by its rigorism, alienated many Christians from holy Communion and from trust in the merciful love of the Redeemer.

Saint Alphonsus Liguori, a most efficacious protagonist against Jansenistic rigorism and coldness of heart, was another great promoter of the devotion to the Sacred Heart and its liturgical celebration. He extols, in particular, God's loving permanent presence in the Eucharist as a sign of the invincible love of the heart of Jesus. He feels that, for those who have received the Body and Blood of Christ with great trust and devotion, the silent proximity of Jesus encourages the eloquent language of love, establishes a perennial memorial of the crucified love, and contributes to a continuous formation of a grateful memory. He sees the daily visit to the Blessed Sacrament[2] as an expression of grateful memory and of constant praise because Jesus never forgets us.

This great eulogist of the eucharistic memorial also considers the human memory to be a basic gift that is superior—in a certain sense—to the intellect and will. Through a grateful memory, God inserts us into the history of salvation, opens to us the treasures of the past, enriches the present, and provides us with the dynamics for future direction.

Finding our blissful abode with Jesus in the Eucharist, indeed in his very heart, helps us to anticipate heaven and provides us with constant guidance on the way to it. In the sacrament of loving union, St. Alphonsus perceives the Divine Physician, the Good Shepherd who nourishes in us effective and faithful responses of friendship, trust, love, and joy in the nearness of his presence.

The most ardent promoters of the liturgical celebration of the mystery of the Sacred Heart have held that this devotion should be seen completely in the light of liturgy, and vice versa. Saint Alphonsus, like other great

---

[2] His astounding work, *Visits to the Blessed Sacrament and Our Lady,* is a favorite resource. A new translation of this perennial favorite was published by Liguori Publications in 2024 in celebration of the National Eucharistic Congress.

venerators of the Sacred Heart, was a persistent promoter of the practice of frequent holy Communion, not only for religious but also equally for lay people in all states of life. He was convinced that rigorists—who, out of respect for the Holy One, as they asserted—did not really know the merciful love of the heavenly Father and the loving heart of the Redeemer.

We do not go to Communion to be rewarded for our virtue. Rather, we joyfully accept the divine invitation because we are aware of the gracious, merciful, and healing love of Jesus and yearn to love him in return. As we receive from him healing and strength, we long all the more to increase our love for him—and, through him, our love for our neighbor—because he alone is the source of redeemed and redeeming love.

In the power of the Holy Spirit, Jesus gives himself in holy Communion with the same love he exhibited when he offered himself up for us on the cross. At the same time, he shares with us the gift of the Spirit to help us return his love and give ourselves totally to him.

We ask him to make us wholly his own and to conform our hearts to his heart. Thus, his consecrating action becomes reality in our lives. We join Jesus in his high-priestly prayer: "For their sake, I now consecrate myself, that they too may be consecrated by the truth" (John 17:19). In confident prayer of supplication, we open ourselves to the rich graces of holy Communion wherein heart reposes in heart.

With hearts renewed, we come closer to the beatitude assured to those who are "pure in heart." A grateful memory will then help us watch over the purity of our motives and intentions.

In the Eucharist, we celebrate the sacrificial love of Jesus—that unsurpassable love that he made visible in his bitter passion and death—while praying that this sacrifice might touch and change our hearts and inspire in us a generous and atoning love. As we praise the Father for having prepared this supreme offering made by Jesus once and forever for all of us, our hearts open more and more to the grace that transforms us and makes us an acceptable offering in union with Christ. Gradually, we learn to free ourselves from everything that stands in the way of our union with the sacrificial and atoning love of Jesus.

In the Eucharist, Jesus prepares a festive banquet for his friends, a pledge of the heavenly banquet and everlasting feast of love and joy. Thus, we come to a better understanding of his invitation: "Come to me, all whose work is hard, whose load is heavy, and I will give you relief" (Matthew 11:28); "Come forward, you who are thirsty; accept the water of life, a free gift to all who desire it" (Revelation 22:17). And we respond with all our hearts: "Come, Lord Jesus" (Revelation 22:20).

Prayers

St. John Henry Newman

O most sacred, most loving heart of Jesus, thou art concealed in the Holy Eucharist, and thou dost beat for us still. Now as then thou sayest, *desiderio desideravi*—"with desire I have desired." I worship thee then with all my best love and awe, with my fervent affection, with my most submissive, most resolved will.

O my God, when thou dost condescend to suffer me to receive thee, to eat and drink thee, and thou for a while takest up thy abode within me, O make my heart beat with thy heart. Purify it of all that is earthly, all that is proud and sensual, all that is hard and cruel, all perversity, all disorder, all deadness. So fill it with thee, that neither the events of the day nor the circumstances of the time may have power to ruffle it. In thy love and thy fear, may it have peace.

Amen.

SAINT ALPHONSUS' *NOVENA TO THE SACRED HEART*

O my Jesus, you have not refused to give me your blood and your life. How, then, can I refuse to give you my miserable heart? Never let that happen! O my dear Redeemer, I give you all my will; accept it and do with it what you will. I have nothing and can do nothing, but this I have to give you—my heart, which you have given me, which nobody can steal from me. I may lose my natural goods, my blood, my life, but not my heart. With this heart, I can love you and will love you.

O my God, teach me to forget myself; teach me how to come to your pure love; in your goodness, you have already inspired in me a great desire for this love. I feel in myself a strong desire to please you.

O loving heart of Jesus, it is now up to you to make wholly yours this poor heart that in the past has been so ungrateful and, which by its own fault, is now empty of your love. Inflame this heart with your love, as your heart burns with love for me. Unite my will wholly with your will so that I shall not will anything not willed by you. From now on, your holy will shall be the rule for all my actions, all my thoughts, all my desires. Lord, I am sure that you will not deny me the grace to live up to this resolution, which I make today at your feet; I resolve to embrace with peace whatever designs you have for me, now and forever.

Amen.

19

LEARNING TO LOVE IN THE HEART OF JESUS

Dwell in me, as I in you. No branch can bear fruit by itself, but only if it remains united with the vine; no more can you bear fruit, unless you remain united with me.

I am the vine, and you the branches. He who dwells in me, as I dwell in him, bears much fruit; for apart from me, you can do nothing. He who does not dwell in me is thrown away like a withered branch. The withered branches are heaped together, thrown on the fire, and burnt.

If you dwell in me, and my words dwell in you, ask what you will, and you shall have it. This is my Father's glory, that you may bear fruit in plenty and so be my disciples. As the Father has loved me, so I have loved you. Dwell in my love. If you heed my commands, you will dwell in my love, as I have heeded my Father's commands and dwell in his love.

I have spoken thus to you, so that my joy may be in you, and your joy complete. This is my commandment: love one another, as I have loved you.

JOHN 15:4–12

LEARNING TO LOVE IN THE HEART OF JESUS

The tender love of Jesus is most personal. It touches everyone in his or her inmost being, in the heart. Yet it may not be privatized. It is an all-out rallying cry. Jesus wants his disciples to learn not only to love him but also to love, with him, all whom he loves and to love them, as it were, with his own loving heart.

Here, we wish to concentrate on a feature of the devotion to the Sacred Heart that has been mentioned time and again: learning to be so much at home in the heart of Jesus that we join him willingly and joyously in his love for all whom his powerful love has created and redeemed.

Our first priority is to learn how to love Jesus, to enter fully into the mystery of his loving heart by loving him in return. This is expressed in the basic command: "Dwell in me." But, immediately and inevitably, there follows the call from the Father to love, with Jesus, his glory in obedience to his glorious command: "Love one another!"

This means joining Jesus and the Father in their liberating, redeeming, and healing love for all humankind. Devotion to the Sacred Heart is essentially the cult of love by which God, in Jesus, has loved us and, at the same time, the exercise of our love for God and love for the rest of humankind.

To allow Jesus to conquer our hearts means to enter into the flow of his love. It implies that we "discard the old nature with its deeds and have put on the new nature, which is being constantly renewed in the image of its Creator and brought to know God" (Colossians 3:9–10). The need for grace follows: "Then put on the garments that suit God's chosen people, his own, his beloved: compassion, kindness, humility, gentleness, patience. Be forbearing with one another, and forgiving, where any of you has cause for complaint: you must forgive as the Lord forgave you. To crown all, there must be love, to bind all together and complete the whole. Let Christ's peace be arbiter in your hearts; to this peace you were called as members of a single body. And be filled with gratitude" (Colossians 3:12–15).

Saint Thérèse of Lisieux (1873–1897) grasped the essence of devotion to the heart of Jesus when she showed her great desire to find her place and role in the Mystical Body by being a loving person in the very heart of Jesus. It is well known that she would have liked to see women ordained as priests, and she wanted to become one of them. But this unfulfilled desire did not upset her, for she arrived at this alternative: more important than all the ministries and charisms in the Mystical Body is total immersion in the propagation and circulation of love that comes from the heart of Jesus and unites us with his loving heart. This should be the positive desire of every priest, religious, and layperson.

We proclaim the love of Jesus in a trustworthy and understanding manner by loving his own as he did. "His own" are his friends, the believers, those who love him.

Those who offend, insult, hate, and persecute his friends drive a lance into Jesus' heart more cruelly than the soldier who, on Mount Calvary, opened Jesus' heart with a lance. Saul—before he became Paul—was doing just that when he was thrown to the ground on the road to Damascus, and a voice from heaven asked, "Saul, Saul, why do you persecute me?" (Acts 9:4)

But the love of Jesus reaches beyond his own. He has come to save sinners. He celebrates the Messianic meal with tax gatherers and "other bad characters." While still on the cross, he prayed for those who had crucified him, for all his enemies. Hence, our devotion to the Sacred Heart becomes sincere and truthful when we learn from Jesus to pardon with healing love and to love the unloving and unloved. Jesus came to save the world from the killing frost of lovelessness.

With gentle love, he meets the unloved and despised and enables them to receive and give love in return. For true devotees of the Sacred Heart, there are no "hopeless cases"—they don't write off anyone. That Jesus' love for us is "costly" is confirmed by his most bitter suffering and the shedding of his precious blood. We cannot effectively enter the redeeming stream of his love for people without being conformed to his sacrificial love, without being ready to suffer for love's sake. Pope Pius XI suggests, as a practical example of this "sacrificial love," a simple lifestyle in constant readiness to assist the poor and unloved.

It is a lifelong task to learn how to love Jesus and to enter into the redeeming stream of his love for all. We should never presume that we have already met the mark. Those who are thoroughly captured by Jesus' love will, like Paul, "Press on, hoping to take hold of that for which Christ once took hold of me....forgetting what is behind me, and reaching out for that which lies ahead" (Philippians 3:12–13).

Knowing Christ lovingly, and lovingly striving for a better knowledge of him, go hand in hand with greater love of neighbor and better perception of the kind of love that can be offered in the name of Jesus. Friends of the heart of Jesus strive for the kind of love of neighbor that Christ can somehow recognize as his own.

Prayer

O most loving heart of Jesus, what a fool I was when I concentrated all my energies on garnering different kinds of knowledge and skills, while I strove with only a divided heart for the real wisdom of knowing you and your way of loving people! I am afraid that I must honestly confess that in this supreme art I have always remained inept. Yet, thanks to your grace, my heart is still able to see my folly and my perverted sense of proportions. I am deeply pained by my lack of understanding, and in this sorrow, I see a sign of your gracious patience and forgiveness. So, with your grace,

I dare to hope that from now on, I shall seek first the reign of your love and all else for your sake.

Yet, because I am rightly afraid of my inconsistency, superficiality, and weakness, I implore you, by your loving heart, to confirm my resolution and to increase my desire to seek first your love and the art of loving people in union with your heart. This I ask, no matter what the price may be.

Reveal to me the meaning of Holy Scripture, so that, like the hearts of the disciples on the road to Emmaus, mine too may burn with love for you and with you. Pour out on all of us your Holy Spirit, that we may become a credible community of disciples, and the world may believe that the reign of love is at hand.

Amen.

20

Union in the Heart of Jesus

The whole body of believers was united in heart and soul.

ACTS 4:32

UNION IN THE HEART OF JESUS

"**It is not for these alone that I pray,** but for those also who through their words put their faith in me; may they all be one: as thou, Father, art in me and I in thee, so also may they be in us, that the world may believe that thou didst send me. The glory which thou gavest me, I have given to them, that they may be one, as we are one; I in them and thou in me, may they be perfectly one. Then the world will learn that thou didst send me, that thou didst love them as thou didst me" (John 17:20–23).

Unity, solidarity, and peace, come from God and lead to him. They are not primarily a matter of organization but of the heart: of the inmost being of people who are able and willing to build bridges between people and, by healthy relationships, can contribute also to the healing of public life.

It is nowhere written that in the apostolic community in Jerusalem, all had the same ideas or all agreed on the solutions to all problems. On the contrary, the Acts of the Apostles tell us that there was partial disagreement on some important questions. But, they were "united in heart and soul." They met each other in the tender and strong love of Jesus, knowing that Jesus loved them all and called them all to share in his redeeming, all-inclusive love. They knew that they were sent for a redemptive witness, which could not exist without their being united in heart and soul.

This unity in heart bore fruit and led to radical approaches in the conduct of community life: no one should suffer misery while others had more than enough; there should be spontaneous and generous sharing; and the poor and widows coming from different cultures should be honored and helped without discrimination. They sought the best possible organizational solutions through gracious dialogue. Everything flowed from their deeply felt solidarity.

John's Gospel leads us to the unfathomable mystery from which such splendid unity of heart and soul arose. The disciples were aware that they were inserted into the supreme mystery of the loving unity between Father and Son. Jesus loves us with the same love as the Father loves us. The Father's love for Jesus is inseparably united with his love for us. In the same way, the love between you and me cannot be separated from the covenanted love of Jesus for his Church, indeed for the whole of humanity, according to the mandate of the Father. This ineffable mystery marks all our Christian life. We are authorized to join Jesus, who calls almighty God "Abba," dear Father, and we are taught by Jesus to call his Father "our Father," thus reminding us that this wonderful prerogative is based on saving solidarity in Christ. We honor the way in which God glorifies his name when we join him and Jesus in an all-embracing unity and love, in mutual respect and concord.

Without sincere effort toward unity in hearts and minds, we can neither hallow the name of the Father nor greet the coming of his kingdom, for we are not yet conformed to his loving will. The Father's will is clearly described for us in the farewell discourses in which Jesus prays that his disciples may be perfectly one, as he and the Father are one. (See John 17:20–23.) Therefore, in prayer taught by Jesus himself and in our life, concord takes top priority.

Unity in heart and mind among adorers of the Sacred Heart of Jesus is not an imperative imposed from outside but a stream of living water, arising from within those who believe and have opened themselves to the Spirit sent by Jesus. It is the expression of our vital insertion into the life of Christ. "Let your bearing toward one another arise out of your life in Christ Jesus" (Philippians 2:5). This is the main perspective and foundation of the counsel imparted to us by Paul: "If then our common life in Christ yields anything to stir the heart, any loving consolation, any sharing of the Spirit, any warmth of affection or compassion, fill up my cup of happiness by thinking and feeling alike, with the same love for one another, the same turn of mind, and a common care for unity" (Philippians 2:1–2).

In his Letter to the Ephesians, Paul's appeal for unity in heart and mind is grounded on the basic truths of our faith: "Be humble always and gentle, and patient too. Be forbearing with one another and charitable. Spare no effort to make fast with bonds of peace the unity which the Spirit gives. There is one body and one Spirit, as there is also one hope held out in God's call to you; one Lord, one faith, one baptism; one God and Father of all, who is over all and through all and in all" (Ephesians 4:2–6).

In this same light, we see the various charisms and

ministries for the building up of the Mystical Body of Christ as described in chapter four of the Letter to the Ephesians. And Paul concludes, "Bonded and knit together by every constituent joint, the whole frame grows through the due activity of each part and builds itself up in love" (Ephesians 4:16). We find the same emphasis and motivation in the First Letter to the Corinthians. All depends on that love that conforms and unites us to Christ and, thus, unites us among ourselves. "Put love first" (1 Corinthians 14:1).

PRAYER

Lord Jesus, most loving and most worthy of love, we thank you for sharing with us—through the Gospel of John to whom you gave the sharp eye of an eagle for the mysteries of your heart—your prayer for unity in heart and mind, so that we might live united with your heart and thus glorify the Father.

O most gracious heart of our Redeemer, you have suffered terribly at the sight of discord among your disciples, their ridiculous rivalry, their jealousy, and their envy for higher positions. And what must your sensitive heart suffer when you see our sloth in matters of mutual love and concord, our laziness in dedicating ourselves to the art of concord in heart and mind, and our failure to learn from you how to love each other as you love us! Forgive us for neglecting to pray zealously for this grace and art, which you earnestly desire to grant to those who pray to you sincerely and unceasingly.

Lord, open our eyes and our hearts so that we may perceive what is essential. Strengthen our resolution to pray, to act, and, when there is need, to suffer for the great cause of unity among your followers.

Amen.

21

Heart of Jesus, the Good Shepherd

I am the Good Shepherd; the Good Shepherd lays down his life for the sheep. The hireling, when he sees the wolf coming, abandons the sheep and runs away, because he is no shepherd, and the sheep are not his. Then the wolf harries the flock and scatters the sheep. The man runs away because he is a hireling and cares nothing for the sheep.

I am the Good Shepherd; I know my own sheep, and my sheep know me—as the Father knows me, and I know the Father—and I lay down my life for the sheep. But there are other sheep of mine, not belonging to this fold, whom I must bring in, and they too will listen to my voice. There will then be one flock, one shepherd. The Father loves me because I lay down my life, to receive it back again.

JOHN 10:11–17

HEART OF JESUS, THE GOOD SHEPHERD

The symbol of the "good shepherd"—and Jesus' testimony to it—found in a culture of shepherds an echo similar to that of the later symbol of the "heart." When the good shepherd speaks, it is really the heart of Jesus speaking. He expresses a kind of mutual knowing between the good shepherd and his sheep, between him and his disciples, which he compares with the loving knowledge between himself and the heavenly Father. It is a knowledge of the heart. The self-giving love of which he speaks is the same love that the pierced heart of Jesus continues to speak from the cross.

Using this same symbol of the good shepherd and emphasizing it in his heart-revealing prayer at the Last Supper, Jesus speaks on the peaceful unity of the redeemed. Both the symbolism of the shepherd and the reality of the loving heart of Jesus, forever beating for us, inspire apostolic zeal and dedication to the cause of peace and unity in all genuine disciples of Christ.

Hesychius describes this point well when he writes, "The apostles are the heart of Jesus, organs of his love." Present-day apostles who "dwell in Jesus' heart," at harmony with his redeeming love, will show a burning zeal for the salvation of all. Knowing the heart and mind of the Good Shepherd and loving with his heart, they can help others to discover their own inner strengths and thereby hear the voice and understand the love of the Redeemer.

After his resurrection, Jesus, the Good Shepherd,

questions Peter three times about his love. Following Peter's humble, stumbling assurance of his love, Jesus—in gracious confirmation of Peter's supreme office as good shepherd—makes the threefold appeal: "Then, tend my lambs, tend my sheep, feed my sheep." Here, Peter is the prototype. All apostolates, all pastoral activity, can be fruitful and truthful only when they arise from humble and loving hearts. Paul expresses this truth in a way that directly reminds us of Jesus' tender love for the redeemed. "God knows how I long for you all, with the deep yearning of Christ Jesus himself" (Philippians 1:8). Another translation reads: "...loving you as Christ Jesus loves you." It is simply impossible to enter intimately into the love of the Redeemer without being seized by his zeal for the salvation of all. This experience of being irresistibly attracted by the intense love of Jesus for all, especially for sinners and those who do not yet know him, has been and still is the basis of many priestly and religious vocations. (I am convinced that we need a strong revival of the devotion to the heart of our Redeemer to overcome the present crisis of priestly vocations.)

But the apostolate of the ministerial priesthood is not the only apostolate. It is the vocation of all believers to be an active part of the Church, which is an apostolic community. Every Christian whose heart is captured by the redeeming love of Jesus will be an apostle in his or her own state in life. Being enraptured by the loving heart of Jesus, the Good

Shepherd, is the necessary key to the apostolate. Thus captivated, we shall bear each other's burdens, encourage and kindly correct one another, and enkindle in many hearts a great enthusiasm for the divine Redeemer and his ongoing work here on earth.

It is an undeniable truth that God knows many ways to lead people to eternal salvation. However, it is a deplorable error to infer from this, as some poorly instructed and superficial Christians do, that apostolic zeal and tireless effort to lead people to the knowledge and love of Christ is not particularly important. We should all seek the profound experience of what it means to "know Jesus," the Good Shepherd, and to be known by him as the Father knows him and he knows the Father. (See John 10:14.) Then, the bliss of such a loving knowledge will make us yearn, as Paul did, with Christ's own love, to bring as many people as possible to the same knowledge, love, and delightful trust in the Good Shepherd.

We cannot really praise God for the full revelation of his love through Jesus, the Good Shepherd, without longing to see God loved and praised by all and to see the joy and peace of those who come to such a saving, liberating knowledge through our cooperation. Jesus, who died for all and is risen for all, considers all people—every man, woman, and child—as his own. If he calls us to share in his love and mission as the Good Shepherd—one who knows his own and wants to lead all into the one flock—then nothing can divert us from the wonderful and urgent vocation to make Jesus known and loved.

Faced with the fact that humankind is exposed to the most atrocious threats of violence, exploitation, hatred, manipulation, and even nuclear destruction, every Christian should realize that humankind needs nothing more urgently than recognition of the saving message of the Good Shepherd who knows how to guide and protect us—if we acknowledge him and entrust ourselves to him.

Why should we not have the courage to warn people into what an abyss they will plunge if they refuse the saving love offered them by Jesus Christ and the Father? If we have not this courage and do not feel the urgency to proclaim the gospel and give witness to it for the salvation of humankind, then we should be disturbed by the realization that we have not yet allowed Christ to captivate us by his love and to conform us to his heart as Good Shepherd.

It is a historical fact that the increase in the devotion to the Sacred Heart during and after the French Revolution led to great apostolic zeal. The members of the many religious congregations dedicated in a special way to the Sacred Heart have been outstanding pioneers in missionary motivation and perseverance during the last two centuries.

Prayer

Lord Jesus, you are the Good Shepherd already foretold in the Old Testament. You have shown us the meaning of the prophecy: "I myself will ask after my sheep and go in search of them. I myself will tend my flock, I myself pen them in their fold, says the Lord God. I will search for the lost, recover the straggler, bandage the hurt, strengthen the sick, leave the healthy and strong to play, and give them their proper food" (Ezekiel 34:11–16).

By doing all this, you have shown us the Father. Your love knows no bounds. Even if we run away and go hopelessly astray, still you want to find us and heal us. O Good Shepherd, make us grateful for such a great love and loving care. Then, gratitude will inspire us to accept generously and joyfully your invitation to share in your mission as good shepherds.

Heart of our Savior, instill your love into the hearts of all who share in the ministry of shepherds in the Church and in the hearts of those whom you have chosen for this sublime vocation. Teach them by your Spirit how to become a true image of you, so that people may come to realize that, in them and through them, you yourself look after them and tend them most lovingly.

In the present crisis of priestly vocations, we pray to you, in your own words, to send workers into your vineyard and to reawaken the spirit of shepherds who are full of enthusiasm and who radiate joy, peace, kindness, and loving care. Give many priests the special charism to discern and encourage priestly vocations and to inspire apostolic zeal in the hearts of the faithful, so that all may realize what a great honor and joy it is to participate in your mission as good shepherds.

Help every husband and wife become for each other a true image of your kind, patient, and healing love. Grant to parents the wisdom and strength to raise their children in your love and to join you in the work of salvation.

Lord Jesus, you have spoken exultantly of those believers who "know" you in a way similar to the way you know the Father. We beg you to grant us from your most loving heart a firm grasp of this essential point, so that we do not desire anything more than to know you lovingly and to grow constantly in this love and knowledge, and thus help each other on the way of salvation.

 *Amen.*

22

Heart of Jesus, the Divine Physician

The Pharisees and the lawyers of their sect complained to his disciples: "Why do you eat and drink," they said, "with tax-gatherers and sinners?" Jesus answered them: "It is not the healthy that need a doctor, but the sick; I have not come to invite virtuous people, but to call sinners to repentance."

LUKE 5:30–32

He [Jesus] went around the whole of Galilee, teaching in the synagogues, preaching the gospel of the kingdom, and curing whatever illness or infirmity there was among the people. His fame reached the whole of Syria, and sufferers from every kind of illness, racked with pain, possessed by devils, epileptic, or paralyzed, were all brought to him, and he cured them.

MATTHEW 4:23–25

HEART OF JESUS, THE DIVINE PHYSICIAN

While the title of "Good Shepherd" is a symbol of abiding care taken from a specific culture, the name "Divine Physician," by which Jesus was honored in early Christianity, is more than a symbol—just as language about the "heart" of Jesus is more than symbolic. These titles signify a deep reality that embraces inexhaustible symbolic riches. Jesus is a healer more so than any human physician. He alone can restore full health and wholeness to body and soul. He is also the most compassionate physician; he was foretold as such by the prophet: "He bore our sufferings, our torments he endured…and by his scourging, we are healed" (Isaiah 53:4–5). From beginning to end, the public activity of Jesus is marked by his healing ministry, reaching its peak in his passion. When taken prisoner, he lovingly healed the ear of the high priest's servant wounded by Peter. (See Luke 22:51.) Hanging on his cross, he healed the heart and soul of the criminal crucified with him. And this is only the prelude. From the pierced heart of our Redeemer flow continual streams of healing graces. The old Germanic word for "Savior" was *Reiland*, and it is still much used. It means the one who brings salvation and healing at the same time. He has come to make us whole and holy.

Jesus is the merciful Samaritan who, faced with the poor man fallen into the hands of robbers, is moved by compassion, takes loving care of him, and does so at his own expense. We all are included in this parable. In the misery of our sins and with all the sufferings that derive from them, we are welcomed by the most compassionate Physician.

Jesus is the healer of those who, with the poisoned lance of their sins, have wounded unto death the healer of us sinners. The wound in his heart, which has become glorious in his resurrection, continues to send forth streams of salvation. Our sins have deserved severe reprisal, but Jesus welcomes us with gentleness, kindness, and healing compassion. His heart, pierced by us, remains open for us as a fountain of salvation.

But his compassion also clearly informs us that healing presumes sincere conversion on our part. How can we be healed if we insist on being strangers to this loving heart instead of turning to him with grateful love? Jesus cannot but hate the sin, since it is an insult against the all-holy Creator and Redeemer. Jesus looks at the sinner as a poor brother or sister who foolishly has wounded himself or herself and has chosen the darkness of exile. He calls the sinner back to wholehearted friendship and offers him or her a new heart, a loving heart, and a grateful memory.

In accord with Christ's mission, proclamation of the Good News and the call to conversion and healing are inseparable. When Jesus proclaims the gospel of the beatitudes as gift and call, a healing power of love "goes out from him." Jesus praying on the mount is a symbol of his absolute union with the Father. This is the source of his healing. But Jesus, being one with the Father, cannot remain distant when he sees our misery. He comes down from the height to heal people who are burdened with guilt and suffering.

This is beautifully expressed by Luke, the physician, in the sermon on the plain: "[Jesus] came down the hill with [the disciples] and took his stand on level ground. There was a great concourse of his disciples and great numbers of people from Jerusalem and Judea and from the seaboard of Tyre and Sidon, who had come to listen to him, and to be cured of their diseases. Those who were troubled with unclean spirits were cured, and everyone in the crowd was trying to touch him, because power went out from him and cured them all" (Luke 6:17–19).

If we are yearning to be freed from self-righteousness, idolatry of status or money, or hardness of heart, and if we desire to be cured of other moral diseases, then we must equally yearn to listen to Jesus and to let the Good News enter our hearts. He who is flooding us with his healing love in the beatitudes also shows us the way to heal hearts, to heal human relationships, and to heal public life.

A decisive condition for being healed and becoming true sharers in Jesus' healing ministry is to conform ourselves to his compassionate love. "How blest are those who show mercy; mercy shall be shown to them" (Matthew 5:7). Jesus teaches us by word and example what true mercy and compassion mean. He told the Pharisees, "Go and learn what that text means, 'I require mercy, not sacrifice.' I did not come to invite virtuous people, but sinners" (Matthew 9:13).

In this context, the expression "virtuous people" means those who meticulously observe certain details of their interpretation of law while looking down on others with disdainful hearts. They are not longing for healing; indeed, they stubbornly turn away from God's healing mercy. They offer unreal sacrifices and refuse the real sacrifice of overcoming their arrogance and renouncing everything that hinders compassionate healing.

By his infinite compassion and merciful actions, Jesus turns our hearts to the heavenly Father: "Be compassionate as your Father is compassionate" (Luke 6:36). With Paul, who has wonderfully experienced God's mercy, we all are to praise "The God and Father of our Lord Jesus Christ, the all-merciful Father, the God whose consolation never fails" (2 Corinthians 1:3).

If our hearts beat at least somewhat in harmony with the heart of Jesus, then we not only will pardon our adversaries from the depths of our hearts but also will try always to welcome them with healing love. This heals our hurt feelings and the memory thereof. However, if we are truly inserted into the compassionate healing ministry of Jesus, we concentrate less on our own needs and more on the needs of others to be healed from hatred and other "evil spirits." This, of course, does not mean that in the process we should be unconcerned about our own state of being, which is a basic good for us and for the Mystical Body of Christ.

Paul gives us an attractive picture of redeemed and

redeeming love when he says, "Love is patient; love is kind and envies no one...[love is] not quick to take offense. Love keeps no score of wrongs" (1 Corinthians 13:4–6). It should be noted that Paul does not say "love must be." Love, flowing from the heart of Jesus and from the heart of the disciple transformed by intimate friendship with Jesus and by the power of the Spirit, is compassionate, is patient. Compassionate and healing thoughts, words, and deeds flow from within those believers who drink thirstily from the fountain of salvation. (See John 7:37–39.) What is important, therefore, is that we turn to Jesus with hearts and minds—that we "dwell in Christ Jesus."

Those touched by the compassionate love of the Redeemer realize from within themselves what these words mean: "If you give to charity, give with all your heart… if you are helping others in distress, do it cheerfully" (Romans 12:8).

Whoever has learned mercy from the loving heart of Jesus has been taught a new understanding of God's saving justice. Such a person will be anguished no longer about his or her own selfish advantage or point of honor, but he or she will hunger and thirst that God's saving justice will prevail. (See Matthew 5:6.)

The encyclical *Dives in Misericordia* (Rich in Compassion) of Pope St. John Paul II is not only a major contribution to a right understanding of the Sacred Heart of Jesus but also an important part of Catholic social doctrine. Those who have learned to praise the God and Father of our Lord Jesus Christ for his compassion and saving justice will commit themselves to work for the solution of the threatening world conflict as both a matter of justice and a matter of compassion. Their compassion will be for the poor, on one hand, but not less for those heartless rich, who just may be the most miserable people on earth. Faced with the contrast that exists between super-affluent societies and the hundreds of millions who die of starvation, their compassion will rest with the poor.

Jesus' mercy extends to all dimensions of human life: the misery of sinfulness, illness of body and mind, extreme poverty, oppression, social disorder. "When he [Jesus] came ashore, he saw a great crowd; and his heart went out to them, because they were like sheep without a shepherd, and he had much to teach them" (Mark 6:34). Surely, people need the Good News above all, but the Gospel does not stop there. It keeps referring to Jesus' teaching. It also tells us that Jesus took care that his listeners had something to eat.

In conformity with the teaching authority of the Church, I steadfastly reject the approach of those who think that liberation and redemption take place mainly or even exclusively through structural changes brought about by economic and political revolution. As Christians, our first requirement is and continues to be the "revolution of being," the healing of hearts and minds, and faith in the resurrection. This does not at all make irrelevant the extreme importance of healing public life through good political planning, good leaders, and our competent participation in shaping wholesome public opinion regarding economic and social conditions.

If, in their innermost being, Christians are conformed to the compassion of Jesus and his hunger and thirst that saving justice prevail, there will arise, on all levels, men and women who will heal public life, including politics.

Prayer

O heart of our Redeemer, you have shown us the Father in his compassion and saving justice. Your heart goes out to all who are in need. We hope to praise your mercy, and that of your heavenly Father, in all eternity. Help us in our commitment to mercy and saving justice in this valley of tears. Let it be the fitting prelude to this praise.

Lord Jesus, we live in a world with many hardened hearts and threatening conflicts. Corruption constantly tempts us, and we cannot deny that we are already partially corrupted. Lord, heal us and make us effective signs of your healing mercy and justice. Divine Savior, send into this estranged world of ours men and women who will straightforwardly bring into it the gospel of mercy and peace.

O heart of Jesus, touch the wealthy, affluent nations, groups, and individuals with a ray of your compassionate love and your zeal for saving justice, so that they may learn what kind of justice you and your heavenly Father want from them.

O meek and powerful heart, you can heal our hearts from coldness and sloth and make us a blessing for many people by our deep repentance and conversion. Lord, let this happen soon!

Amen.

23

JESUS, OUR HUMBLE-HEARTED IDEAL

On that day...I will rid you of your proud and arrogant citizens, and never again shall you flaunt your pride on my holy hill. But I will leave in you a people afflicted and poor. The survivors in Israel shall find refuge in the name of the Lord.

ZEPHANIAH 3:11–12

JESUS, OUR HUMBLE-HEARTED IDEAL

At that time, Jesus spoke these words: "I thank thee, Father, Lord of heaven and earth, for hiding these things from the learned and wise, and revealing them to the simple. Yes, Father, such was thy choice. Everything is entrusted to me by my Father; and no one knows the Son but the Father, and no one knows the Father but the Son and those to whom the Son may choose to reveal him.

"Come to me, all whose work is hard, whose load is heavy; and I will give you relief. Bend your necks to my yoke, and learn from me, for I am gentle and humble-hearted; and your souls will find relief" (Matthew 11:25–29).

Pride and arrogance constrict human hearts and destroy bridges between people. Indeed, they tend to undermine all saving bridges. Pride is the incendiary bomb that destroys hearts and the earth. It is the final cause of the heartless devastation resulting from lovelessness and injustice.

Our humble-hearted Savior guides us in the healing of wounded hearts, of painful memories, of alienated relationships, and difficult human conditions. He builds bridges on which heart discovers heart. The Eternal Word of the Father chose the path of humility in becoming "One-of-us." He did not come with earthly power and glory but was born in the misery of a stable under the sign of a Mother most humble. Saint Augustine writes, "He who can do great things suffers hunger and thirst. He is impoverished. He is made captive, is beaten, crucified, and murdered....He shows us the way: walk in humility, and you will inherit eternity."

Jesus washes the feet of his disciples, knowing well how much they and we need such an example. And the glorified Lord continues to be the great sign of saving humility in the sacraments of faith. He speaks to our hearts and performs his miracles of grace through the humble, earthly signs of the sacraments. Hidden under the sacramental signs, his almighty love is close at hand. In these signs, he continues his humble meeting with us poor sinners until the final revelation of his glory.

What astounding yet sublime love! Almighty God reveals himself in the starkest humility, beginning with his Incarnation and continuing through to the ignominy of the cross. "The divine nature was his from the first" (Philippians 2:6), yet he makes himself the servant of all. In Jesus' humility, almighty God has shown us the absolute boundlessness of the power of his love.

But one thing remains forever intolerable to God: he cannot accept pride and arrogance in creatures. "The arrogant of heart and mind he has put to rout...but the humble have been lifted high" (Luke 1:51–52).

In his prayer of self-revelation as the Son, Jesus praises the Father for revealing himself to the humble-hearted. In his true humanity, Jesus is the embodiment of the humble ones. "No one knows the Father but the Son," and the Son cannot but choose the same road. The humble-hearted will know him and, through him, the Father. Only the humble ones let God be God in all their lives.

Only if we affirm Jesus as the Servant-Messiah can we be healed from the deadly plague of pride. Otherwise, we cannot share in Christ's loving knowledge of the Father.

For many people, God seems to be unreal, far away; in silence, he seems to be hiding himself. Often, one of the reasons for this is that these people's own pride causes them to center in on themselves, thus keeping themselves aloof. They become enemies to others and unbearable burdens to themselves.

Jesus calls us; he reaches out to us in our alienation and self-made exile: "Come to me!" In his compassion, he yearns to free us from the plague of pride and from the blindness that reflects the pride of the world and our own pride. To "bend our necks under his yoke" denotes a faithful "yes" to his humble heartedness, which is an essential dimension of his being and his mission. His humility is the road that divine love takes from celestial glory to our lowliness. It is Jesus' way to our hearts and the astonishing revelation of his heart. It is also the signpost for our journey on the road to redemption and to everlasting life with God.

By his humility, the Redeemer shows us how to find rest for our hearts and how to become a source of peace, kindness, and heartfelt compassion for many people. We begin our learning process with acts of thankfulness and praise for the amazing humility shown by the Son of God made Son of Man, the "One-of-us." Our next step is to generate a profound shame for our own pride and vanity. Our amazement at and gratitude for his humility engender within us a heartfelt sorrow as well as a feeling of relief and renewed trust.

As believers, our basic requirement is to find the courage to learn from Jesus the supreme art of loving humility and humble love, whatever the cost.

Humility comes to Christ's disciples not as a kind of imposition but as a liberation. Christ-like love is humble; we learn this from the heart of Jesus. Therefore, it is evident that we can learn gentleness and humility not apart from love but only as a substantial dimension of love. The more we love Jesus, the more his secret of humility becomes accessible to us; the more eagerly we learn humility and gentleness, the more Jesus can reveal to us the mysteries of his heart.

He can show us the Father and teach us adoration in spirit and truth. Gradually, then, we find peace for our souls and experience ever more the blessings of humility for ourselves and for others.

In today's world, humility speaks a foreign language—but it is the mother tongue in the kingdom of Christ. Happy are those who dare to hear it, to learn it, to speak it, and to give thanks with it and for it.

Prayer

My dear Lord and Savior, I come to you burdened and oppressed by many worries and exhausting labor, by an unbearable yoke that I have imposed on myself because of my lack of humility. It is a burden that I have deserved, but it is also the heavy yoke of a sinful world, of collective pride and arrogance. We are bound together in this lamentable condition. I groan and sigh, realizing my plight in this double slavery of mine and of the world. What relief I find when I listen to your invitation: "Come to me, all whose load is heavy." Yes, now I dare to come.

The more I meditate on the crushing burdens you have carried in your humility, accepting even the most atrocious humiliation from proud and arrogant human beings, the more I am filled with grateful wonder. In your divine glory and your human humility, you are totally Other, so different from the closed-minded and high-handed sons and daughters of Adam. You are the wholly Other, the only true God, so unlike manmade gods. You have come into the valley of tears, where misery is constantly multiplied by humankind's ridiculous pride. You come with an astonishing remedy: the humility of the Son of God, of the Redeemer, who freely has made himself "One-of-us" in all things except sin—the totally holy and humble One.

You come to us whose vanity and pride are intolerable. You come on the royal road of humility, showing us that this is the way to you and to the heart of the Father, the way to the hearts of our fellow human beings, and the way of salvation.

Humble heart of our divine Master, I enroll myself in your school. I want to learn from you, day by day, the royal way of humility. Your love will be my teacher.

Lord, transform our hearts, make them mirror images of your own heart. Make them fountains of healing for many. Lord, make us humble.

Amen.

24

LOVE CONQUERS ALL

What can separate us from the love of Christ? Can affliction or hardship? Can persecution, hunger, nakedness, peril, or the sword? "We are being done to death for thy sake all day long," as Scripture says, "we have been treated like sheep for slaughter"—and yet, in spite of all, overwhelming victory is ours through him who loved us. For I am convinced that there is nothing in death or life, in the realm of spirits or superhuman powers, in the world as it is or the world as it shall be, in the forces of the universe, in heights or depths—nothing in all creation that can separate us from the love of God in Christ Jesus our Lord.

ROMANS 8:35–39

LOVE CONQUERS ALL

Love is the only absolute power in heaven and on earth. For God is Love, and his salvation plan for the world is wholly a design of love. But salvation becomes effective only when we gratefully receive and respond to divine love. This freest gift of God cannot be forced upon any person.

Praised be God, Love found its most perfect dwelling place on earth in the heart of the God-Man, Jesus Christ. The Word of God became flesh to bring us Love from above and, in the name of humankind, to give the response of perfect love. Jesus came to win us over to love's salvific cause. Though wounded and abused by all the lovelessness and hatred in humanity, the heart of Jesus has proved itself victorious against all assaults and has brought home to the Father humankind's thankful love.

To his last heartbeat, Jesus fought for love's victory. The most violent resistance of this sinful world against liberating love could not but conspire to make love's triumph on the Savior's cross even more glorious and evident. Crucified, Jesus prays for his torturers and slanderers. Humiliated by the spiteful plan to crucify him with two common criminals, he makes one of them the first to be brought home by him to the eternal celebration of the victory of love.

The group of those faithful ones who stood beneath Jesus' cross was, indeed, painfully small. But in Mary, his Mother, the new Eve, in the pious and compassionate women and the loving John, there appeared the first pattern of the new family of Jesus, believers in the triumph of love. They saw Jesus' heart, pierced by the soldier's lance, flooding the sinful world with the saving bath of water and blood. And after Jesus' resurrection, they were privileged to see the glory of his opened heart. Thomas was even allowed to touch it with his hand. For him and for all believers, this heart is the great sign of God's victory and the sure promise of final conquest.

Faith tells us that love is triumphant in its total gift of self. The redeemed find their true selves when they leave behind their selfish selves in the total service of love.

At the very moment when Jesus reached the most abject point of humiliation and disdain, he was already exalted in and for the victory of his all-embracing love. He had begun to draw to his heart all those whom the Father had given him.

The firm and faithful hope for love's final conquest constitutes the very substance of Christianity. It is not worthwhile to dedicate one's life for any cause inferior to that of love or to work hard for anything that is not inspired by redeeming love and does not serve its cause. But the cause of love for which Christ came is, indeed, worth all dedication and even all suffering. This is the one precious pearl that is worth more than all else. The reward for those who have given everything away for love's sake is now the down payment on nothing less than love itself, the abode of love for all eternity.

This victorious love is not our invention or our achievement. It is unqualified grace, an undeserved gift flowing from the heart of the Redeemer. But love looks for grateful hearts that are ready to enrich the hearts of others.

There is nothing we can pray for with greater confidence than for this love. The heart of Jesus is the certain assurance that he himself is longing to bestow on us this best of all his gifts. We ask for it in humble and persevering prayer, for we can receive it only if we recognize God as God, the source and goal of all love, and recognize how much we need this absolutely undeserved gift. Praying for this love that conquers all, we encounter the inmost longing of the heart of Jesus and, indeed, of the heavenly Father, beseeching them to pour out on all believers this precious gift.

As children of Adam and creatures of a harsh world, we are narrow-minded and locked into our selfish selves. But, newly born of grace and trusting completely in God, we can say with Paul, "I have strength for anything through him who gives me power" (Philippians 4:13). To pray, thus, is to pray for the supreme and all-embracing gift of redeeming love, for perseverance in learning this noblest art, and for our share in the final victory of love.

If love does not take first place in all our prayers and endeavors, then our struggles are impotent in the warfare between vice and virtue. But if our hearts yearn for this water of life, then even our weaknesses cannot frighten us. We know that our power to conquer comes from God alone. (See 2 Corinthians 4:7.)

The final victory of love is expressly foreshadowed for us if we love those who are unloved as well as those who offend or despise us, if we sow love where there is hatred, and if we strive to win others to the reign of love visible in the heart of Jesus.

This victory, involving as it does the conquest of our deeply rooted selfishness and entanglement in collective selfishness, is the victory of faith bearing fruit in love. The greatest work of God, in and through those who hope for everything from him, is love. "Everything" means nothing less than unending participation in love's victory.

Prayer

Most loving Master, your heart is the trophy of history's greatest triumph. The surge of hatred is thwarted by your love. All who refuse your love are like chaff blown away by the wind; yet you do not even write them off. As long as they live, you will seek them and invite them to the banquet celebrating your love for them.

O divine heart filled with love, you have won my heart. You have dilated it, enlivened it, and enriched it with your most powerful gift, your gracious and attractive love. To you, I entrust myself.

The world seeks to entice me with dreams of success, achievements, and other vain conquests. Help me to be vigilant in the fight against these seductions.

Grant me wisdom, so that I may have only one thing in mind: the victory of your love in my heart, in my conduct, and in the world around me.

It is good that I had to experience my own painful weakness, for now nothing remains to me but to put all my trust in you. If I realize and acknowledge fully that I can do nothing in the realm of saving love but long for it with all my heart and pray for it, then I may not doubt that I shall be admitted to the triumphal procession of those who eternally celebrate with you the victory of your love in us.

My Savior, everybody needs love; everyone's heart is made for abiding love. Your saving love needs witnesses whose hearts have become fountains of its "living water." Lord, help us to become ever more "light for the world." Increase in us faith in your love and trust in its final victory.

Amen.

25

LOVE SETS US FREE

Turning to the Jews who had believed in him, Jesus said, "If you dwell within the revelation I have brought, you are indeed my disciples; you shall know the truth, and the truth will set you free." They replied, "We are Abraham's descendant; we have never been in slavery to any man.

"What do you mean by saying, 'You will become free men'?" "In very truth I tell you," said Jesus, "that everyone who commits sin is a slave. The slave has no permanent standing in the household, but the son belongs to it forever. If then the Son sets you free, you will indeed be free."

JOHN 8:31–36

In one of her letters, St. Margaret Mary Alacoque describes the devotion to the Sacred Heart as response to "the desire of the heart of Jesus to tear all men away from the reign of Satan and to bring them home into the sweet freedom of the reign of his love." This expresses accurately what Jesus says in the eighth chapter of John.

There are two great questions that perturb all thinking people today: "What is truth?" and "What is true freedom?" The two are inseparable. Jesus came to reveal by his being, his actions, his word, and finally by his death and resurrection the saving and liberating truth. In a completely new way, he has restored to humankind the original gift of freedom. The renewed freedom of the redeemed receives its meaning and strength from the love of Christ.

Probably the oldest known Christian hymn (found in Philippians 2:6–11) is a liturgical praise of the amazing liberty of the Son of God, who, in divine freedom, "made himself nothing, assuming the nature of a slave." The hymn points to Christ's resurrection, which finally reveals that unique freedom and the dynamics of love. "Therefore, God raised him to the heights and bestowed on him the name above all names."

So, we learn from Jesus' heart what true freedom is and what it is not.

Proud people claim freedom for themselves as if it were their own capital that should pay interest to them alone. They try to extend their freedom by rebelling against the

One who has entrusted it to them. But this stolen, falsely claimed freedom proves to be only a one-way, no-exit street to self-slavery.

How different is the freedom of Jesus! He sees himself and his freedom as gifts from the Father, and in gratitude he freely gives himself back in purest love and loving service. His freedom in being One with the Father proves to be the source of boundless freedom to love us poor sinners with divine and human love. By our sinfulness, we are the unloved and unloving, but thanks to the absolute freedom of Christ, we know that we are loved. By the power of his Spirit, we can share in his love for the Father and for our brothers and sisters.

The self-giving love of Jesus is the great historical event of liberation. In his full humanity, Jesus "fulfills" the new law of liberty—the perfect law of love—by the power of the Holy Spirit. By the same power, he enables believers to live on the same level of freedom. Paul dramatically describes the difference: The unredeemed apprehend themselves as prisoners "under the law"—that is, in their "bodily members." They are people "under the law of sin," slaves of their own sinfulness and the world's sin-solidarity. Such a poor sinner can only cry out, "Miserable creature that I am, who is there to rescue me out of this body doomed to death?" (Romans 7:24). But the response of the redeemed, who know that they were slaves "to the law of sin" because of their selfish selves, can be only never-ending praise of

God, who alone has set us free "through Jesus Christ our Lord! Thanks be to God!" (Romans 7:25).

This freedom is not a sterile concept or an unattainable ideal. It is a new life "because in Christ Jesus the life-giving law of the Spirit has set you free from the law of sin and death" (Romans 8:2). With the new life comes a new outlook. "Those who live on the level of the Spirit have the spiritual outlook, and that is life and peace" (Romans 8:6).

People who are deluded by their own selfish selves live in constant contradiction to their true selves as intended by the Creator. They live at enmity with the rest of the world and are a curse to themselves and to others, whom they try to lead into the same slavery and the same perverted outlook on "freedom."

Paul describes the freedom of the children of God in few but eloquent words: "Everything belongs to you…yet you belong to Christ, and Christ to God!" (1 Corinthians 3:22–23). If we entrust ourselves to Christ as he entrusted himself to the Father, we are at home in his loving heart. We share his liberating outlook. We are free for each other and can enjoy all the gifts of God as signs of his love—gifts destined also to become signs of mutual love. To live on this level is what the Old Testament prophets foretold under the symbol of "a new heart."

If we accept that freedom of Christ by which he entrusted himself to his Father in the service of all—thus glorifying the name of the Father—then we shall be free from agonizing slavery. We learn to serve God out of grateful love and not out of fear of punishment. "God is love; he who dwells in love is dwelling in God, and God in him. This is for us the perfection of love, to have confidence on the day of judgment, and this we can have, because even in this world we are as he is. There is no room for fear in love; perfect love banishes fear" (1 John 4:16–17).

Many people in today's world are so addicted to selfish freedom that they refuse any covenant of faithfulness. Of course, they, too, want to talk of love, but only of a love "free" to be unstable. Christ has been faithful unto death and thus has called us into the new and eternal covenant of faithful love. One who has found one's life and abode in Jesus is free for a wholehearted "Yes! Here I am! call me!" Having put our trust in the faithful One, we implore and receive the gifts of faithful love and courageous allegiance in the service of love. In this way, we can set out in saving solidarity on the road to the eternal kingdom of freedom.

Jesus' freedom is not only a "freedom to be" but the supreme "freedom to be for others"— the freedom of the Savior of the world. If, with Christ, we have conformed our will to God's will, then, by grace, we can rejoice in the "freedom of the children of God." This is a source of joy for all of creation "because the universe itself is to be freed from the shackles of mortality and enter upon the liberty and splendor of the children of God. Up to the present, we know, the whole created universe groans in all its parts as if in the pangs of childbirth" (Romans 8:21–23). Our growth in solidaric freedom is in the interest of the world, for which we are meant to be, in Christ and through him, a shining light.

Having entrusted ourselves to Christ, we are also freed from fear of death. If we live in Christ, "death is gain" (Philippians 1:21). The more we find our abode in Jesus' heart, the greater will be our joy when he calls us to be with him forever.

The measure of our freedom arises from the measure of our lives with Jesus in response to his boundless love and from our union with him in his love for the Father and for the redeemed.

Christian freedom is a light enkindled by the fire of Christ's own love. Inflamed by Jesus' love and inspired by his life, we live lives of service to our neighbor and the world. All our commitments to external freedom—to economic, cultural, social, and political structures that favor people's freedom—will have effective and lasting results only to the extent that they arise out of our love for Christ.

Prayer

Most loving heart of Jesus, burning hearth of sacrificial love, we worship you and join you in praising the Father for the greatest and all-embracing gift of love. Created by and for your love, O Eternal Word of the Father, we have received plenteous redemption, which enables us to love you and, with you, our sisters and brothers in the freedom of adopted children of God. We praise you and the Father, in the Holy Spirit, for your infinite freedom to love us so much.

We, members of sinful humanity, have dishonored your great gift of freedom, because we did not render thanks for it. In our foolishness, we set out to test and prove our own freedom, even in rebellion against your loving will. In this false freedom, we left your Father's house to go into exile and self-imposed slavery—a slavery that we prolong every time we use our freedom against you, the Giver of all good gifts. Our punishment for this is that, as miserable slaves of perverted self-love, we place ourselves in the position of becoming unable to love you.

O Word of the Father, breathing the Spirit of love from all eternity, in fulfillment of the saving design of the Father, you shouldered our miseries except the greatest one: the incapacity for true love. Yet, our incapacity has made you suffer more than any other human being could suffer, and you have done this out of compassion, in unrestricted freedom to "bear our burden." We can never marvel enough at your boundless love for us sinners. You welcome us with the same freedom you bestowed on the poor woman of Samaria, restoring her to dignity and to redeemed love. What more could you have done to convey on us the freedom of the children of God!

O source of all freedom and love, open our eyes. Help us to understand that all talk and effort for liberation are in vain, unless we gratefully allow you to make us free for your love. Help us to seek first the kingdom of this loving freedom. Thus, we pray, O Lord, make us free!

Amen.

26

Heart of Jesus and the Paschal Mystery

First and foremost, I handed on to you the facts which had been imparted to me: that Christ died for our sins, in accordance with the scriptures; that he was buried; that he was raised to life on the third day, according to the scriptures.

1 Corinthians 15:3–4

"Death is swallowed up; victory is won!" "O death, where is your victory? O death, where is your sting?" The sting of death is sin, and sin gains its power from the law, but God be praised, as he gives us the victory through our Lord Jesus Christ.

Therefore, my beloved brothers, stand firm and immovable, and work for the Lord always, work without limit, because you know that in the Lord your labor cannot be lost.

1 Corinthians 15:55–58

HEART OF JESUS AND THE PASCHAL MYSTERY

The **Passover feast of the Old Testament** has found its fulfillment in the passage of Jesus through the Red Sea of suffering and death, culminating in the victory of the resurrection, the triumph of love. His death is a totally new event, transforming the meaning of death for believers. It becomes Pascha, the passing-over to the fullness of life.

The mystery of redemption is Christ himself in his Passover. In this, he is revealed as the One who is "consecrated and sent into the world by the Father" (John 10:36). Not only has he wrought redemption; he himself is our wisdom and our virtue, our holiness and our freedom. (See 1 Corinthians 1:30.) In his death, Jesus is totally seized and consecrated by the holiness of the heavenly Father. He is the forever-accepted sacrifice, the abiding intercessor for the redeemed. The wound in his heart remains not as a painful laceration but as the open fountain of salvation for all who turn to him.

Jesus' death is the supreme prayer, adoration in spirit and truth, manifestation of trust and love, sacrifice of praise and intercession. Hence, living in Christ and dying with Christ (as one unit) becomes the Christian way of prayer—total openness for the living water flowing from the heart of Jesus.

Saint Augustine writes, "God wants our yearning to be awakened so that we can receive what he desires to grant us. For God is great, but our capacity to receive is small and miserly. Therefore, we are challenged: 'widen your hearts!'"

Jesus longs intently to impart to us the riches of his redemption. His heart is opened wide for us. His death has been the supreme fulfillment of his intercession for us, and its acceptance by the Father is sealed by Christ's resurrection. Thus, the heart of the risen and glorious Christ is the abiding assurance that the Father, wanting to lead us through death and resurrection to our final home, urgently invites us to conform ourselves with the prayer of Jesus.

The evangelists inform us that Jesus died at three o'clock in the afternoon. In Israel, this was the privileged hour of prayer, of the evening sacrifice in the temple. From that point in time, Jesus took over as the never-ending hour of prayer and the acceptable sacrifice.

This sheds abundant light on what is meant by prayer "in the name of Jesus." We pray truly in his name if we widen our hearts to conform to the will of the Father as Jesus did and if, out of love for God and neighbor, our persevering prayer becomes an all-embracing desire for the redemption of all. Believers must find their abode in Jesus' heart, longing to pray as he prayed—indeed, longing to become prayer as he did to pray truly "in the name of Jesus."

His compassionate and interceding love for us continues to such an extent in the risen Lord that he wants to absorb us and make us a part of his love. To this end, we consecrate ourselves to the heart of Jesus so that he can fill us with his redeeming love.

The paschal mystery of the death and resurrection of Christ is the center and heart of salvation history. Hence, it should be the center of our own lives. The basic dimensions of being at home in Jesus' heart and thus in his paschal mystery are as follows:

Grateful remembrance of Jesus' painful Passover through the sea of suffering and praise for his having become forever our intercession—"our holiness and freedom"—thereby allowing the past to impress on our memory all that the Lord has done for us.

Living in the presence of Jesus here and now, in vigilance and openness to him who has come; who comes here and now to prepare us for his final coming and to enable us to be dedicated to his reign.

Hope-filled expectation and clear direction on our road to final homecoming in the heart of our Redeemer. Paul describes the life to come as being at home with the Lord. (See 2 Corinthians 5:6–9.) If we are so much at home in this world that we do not long for our final abode with the Lord, this is a sign of a love of God that is still too weak. From the beginning, Jesus himself cared about our abiding with him: "Father, I desire that these men, who are thy gift to me, may be with me where I am, so that they may look upon my glory, which thou hast given me before the world began" (John 17:24).

In a moving symbol of heartfelt friendship, Scripture enables us to consider our lives in Christ as an invitation to the eternal banquet of love and bliss. We are Jesus' invited guests, "friends of the bridegroom." The celebration of the Eucharist and visitation of the Blessed Sacrament remind us of this nearness to Christ and thus strengthen a grateful memory and watchful readiness.

If we live up to our insertion into salvation history with Christ—by grateful remembrance of past benefits, watchful readiness for present opportunities, and sound foresight for the coming life—then the Lord will grant us special gifts to make this journey for which Christ is both our way and our goal: the gifts of discernment, serenity, and, above all, peace and joy in his love.

Prayer

O my loving Redeemer, most worthy of all my love, I feel a deep longing for a most intimate union with you, yet I know that your desire to see me totally united with you is infinitely greater, because it is the expression of pure love. And while my desire is still marked by inconstancy, your wish to grant me the full experience of your friendship is constant and faithful. Lord, purify and strengthen my longing for total love and dedication to you. Widen my heart! Fill it with your love!

We thank you, divine Master, for fully activating

praise, thanksgiving, and intercession in our name. Send forth your Spirit, transform us, and help us to be so united with you that we can truthfully pray in your name.

Lord, help me to overcome the distractions caused by my superficiality. Grant me a grateful memory so that I can faithfully meditate on all that you have done and suffered for me. Awaken me from my lethargy and let me no more forget that you have written me and all humankind into your loving memory. Lord, help me to be vigilant, ready, and able to recognize your coming and your invitation to join you. Give me keen eyes to see more clearly the steps I must take to reach my final goal.

Fill my heart with supreme confidence in your graciousness. Give me serenity in the vicissitudes of life. Make me long to be forever at home with you and the Father in your heavenly kingdom.

Lord, make me one with your Passover so that I can look forward to the hour of my death, my passover into our abiding home. Free me from anguish and slavish fear. Grant me the grace of perseverance and joyful acceptance when you come to call me home to you.

Amen.

27

Heart of Jesus, Source of All Joy

The Lord is my refuge and defense
  and has shown himself my deliverer.
And so you shall draw water with joy from the springs
  of deliverance.
You shall all say on that day:
Give thanks to the Lord and invoke him by name,
Make his deeds known in the world around....
Sing psalms to the Lord, for he has triumphed, and
  this must be made known in all the world.
Cry out, shout aloud, you that dwell in Zion,
For the Holy One of Israel is among you in majesty.

ISAIAH 12:2–6

The liturgy of the Sacred Heart of Jesus is, above all, an invitation to joy in the Lord. Jesus wants to see us rejoice in his love. To overlook or minimize this dimension would be to falsify the devotion. The words of Isaiah 12:2, "You shall draw water with joy," are the first words of the Sacred Heart encyclical promulgated by Pope Pius XII. And the first antiphon of the office of reading for this feast is: "With you, O Lord, is the fountain of life, from your delightful stream you give us to drink."

If we truly believe in the wholly divine and, at the same time, wholly human love of Jesus, and we truly believe in our being invited to the banquet of love and joy in our eternal abode in Jesus' heart, then surely our hearts exult for joy. Everyday small troubles will not deprive us of our serenity and peace if our hearts are joyful. Indeed, all our personal sufferings are trifling compared with the love that the Lord has manifested to us and the happiness that he holds out to us.

The second psalm read at the Office of Readings for this feast is a hymn of joy and an invitation to rejoice: "Sing to the Lord a new song, for he has done wondrous deeds. The Lord has made his salvation known. Sing joyfully to the Lord, all you lands; break into song; sing praise. Let the rivers clap their hands, the mountains shout with them for joy."

Lovers find their joy in their mutual love and presence to each other. How much greater must be our joy to know that he, who by nature is Love and has shown us his boundless love, really longs for our love in return. Indeed, he is far more interested in our love than in our deeds. He surely wants good deeds also, but mainly as signs and fruit of our grateful love.

What is done with love and for love's sake, with the firm assurance that it pleases the Beloved, is done devotedly; the burden is scarcely felt. When good friends meet each other, heart speaks to heart, and they find joy in each other. So, too, whoever is seized by the heartfelt love of Jesus turns to him with joy and is happy to thank him and praise him.

In this light, we can better understand why great venerators of the Sacred Heart, such as St. John Eudes, St. Margaret Mary Alacoque, and St. Alphonsus, were so eager to promote the liturgical celebration of its feast. They all recognized in their hearts that the eucharistic celebration is joyous thanksgiving and praise for the great love God has manifested to us in Jesus. Therefore, they saw that the mystery of the inexhaustible love of Jesus' heart is a special reason for joyful celebration. Their desire was to have a special feast that would call people's attention to this joyous dimension of the mystery of redemption.

For one who truly venerates the Sacred Heart, it is unthinkable to consider the Sunday Mass as a mere exercise of duty. Rather, it is an immeasurable privilege to be near to the Lord, to be assured of his coming to us in love. It is a supreme joy to join Christ so intimately in the praise of the Father.

The renewed liturgy is marked by this joyous praise of God, but this does not mean we need no longer pay special attention to our own personal love of Jesus' heart. Liturgy needs the joy that comes from the depths of our hearts, nourished by the heartfelt love of Jesus. The pious Israelites joyfully sang their pilgrim songs on the way to the temple. How great, then, must be our joy when we experience in faith the ineffable love with which Jesus contacts us in the Eucharist and in so many other saving signs of redemption! The dynamics of the life of the Church and of our own lives bring us closer to the Lord.

This is our abiding and ever-increasing joy. "I rejoiced when they said to me, 'Let us go to the house of the Lord'" (Psalm 122:1). This eucharistic, thankful, and joyous love of Jesus transforms all our lives into a happy pilgrimage to our eternal home, with the Lord leading us toward a hope-filled homecoming. Friendship with Jesus here on earth is both a "being with" and a "living with" Christ; it establishes a wholesome tension between the now and the not-yet. Christ has taken hold of us; he draws us closer to his heart. The initial joy, great as it is, makes us look forward to its fulfillment when heart will repose in heart forever.

Prayer

Why are you downcast, my soul, why do you sigh within me? Despite my sinfulness and weakness, I have enough reasons to be consoled, even to rejoice, for I can still praise you, my dearest Lord. It is right that I weep because of my sins, but it is more fitting to rejoice because even my past sins tell me to praise your merciful love with all my heart. And why? Because you have forgiven me. My very pain—that I came so late to love you—is one more sign that you do not take away from me your loving kindness.

All of creation and the whole history of salvation tell me of your great love for us. The joyful and serene countenances of people who love you tell me with no need for words: learn to love Jesus, learn it better every day, and your heart will overflow with happiness and will radiate peace.

If I see priests and religious with sour faces, I would like to ask them to go into hiding until they have found joy again in you, dear Lord. Help them to realize how absurd it is for those who know you to allow trifles to disturb them and to be embittered by small offenses. Compassionate Savior, help them to seek and find all their joy in you.

Jesus, I thank you for allowing me so often to meet people who, in the midst of most painful suffering, radiate joy and peace—people who so convincingly invite others to praise you. You offer your love as source of joy and peace to all who sincerely seek you.

O divine Physician, heal us of all self-induced sadness. Let us drink joyfully from your springs of salvation!

Lord, let your countenance shine upon us! Send us your light and your truth. Make us wise enough to seek joy at the purest fountain, your heart.

We are thirsty for your love, and we come to you. Let us drink as you promised, so that streams of living water will flow from within us. Send us your Holy Spirit and make us joyous messengers of your blissful love!

Amen.

28

HEART OF JESUS, HUMAN SYMBOL OF DIVINE LOVE

At his coming into the world, [Jesus] says, "Sacrifice and offering thou didst not desire, but thou hast prepared a body for me. Whole-offerings and sin-offerings thou didst not delight in." Then I said, "Here am I: as it is written of me in the scroll, I have come, O God, to do thy will."

HEBREWS 10:5–7

"**Destroy this temple,**" Jesus replied, "and in three days I will raise it again." They said, "It has taken forty-six years to build this temple. Are you going to raise it again in three days?" But the temple he was speaking of was his body.

After his resurrection, his disciples recalled what he had said, and they believed the Scripture and the words that Jesus had spoken (John 2:19–22).

At the time when Christ came upon the scene, the great world religions, as well as the mainstreams of philosophy, showed great disdain for the human body. Early Christianity had to face this problem. In answer, the biblical texts are strong and clear. Christ's true humanity, including its bodily dimension, belongs to the foundations of our faith. The dignity of the human body appears both in Christ's sacrifice on the cross and in his resurrection.

From the beginning, Jesus praises the Father for his body; it is a gift of the Father. In his body, Jesus is consecrated to do the Father's will. While the Letter to the Hebrews emphasizes that the true Body of Christ brings to an end all kinds of sacrificial offerings in John's Gospel, Jesus himself sees in his body, which is to be offered for humankind, the real temple. The bodily reality has much to do with the worship "of God in spirit and truth" (John 4:24).

True, "God is Spirit," but he lets his glory shine in his visible works, of which the human body is his masterpiece, the embodiment of spirit. In his or her bodily reality, the human person is to manifest visibly his or her being created in the image and likeness of God. In Jesus, the body and the physical heart become privileged realities in the work of redemption.

On the cross, Jesus reveals himself as embodied freedom in the act of supreme love and trust. He offers his life—"his body," in biblical language—as the greatest gift received from the Father and the greatest offering to be brought to the Father for humankind. In the hour of his death, Jesus' body becomes the real temple wherein God is adored, and his loving heart is the Holiest of Holies in this temple.

Through his battered body and his heart widely opened for us, Jesus makes visible and tangible his love for us and for his Father. Nailed on the cross, his arms reach out for all. This body and this heart build bridges between heaven and earth and between person and person.

This crucified body is the acceptable sacrifice, not because of the bitter pains it has to suffer, but because of the love that shines through, even in this cruel death. It is "the body given up for us," and Jesus wants to be sure that every believer throughout the ages not only will be reminded of this but also will come in contact with this body given up for him or her.

And after having served in the work of redemption, Jesus' body is not hidden away. It is raised to glory and is the perennial gift to the Father and, at the same time, a gift to all believers. In his body, Jesus has fullness of life; while giving up this body for humankind, he receives the greatest glory, which shines in it eternally. So, he can say, "I am the resurrection and I am life" (John 11:25).

We are "the body of Christ." This paradigm has rich and realistic meaning. We enter the covenant between Christ and his Church with our full bodily reality: not only with intellect, memory, and will but also with affections, feelings, and emotions. All these dimensions are "embodied."

The body of Christ—having become the real "temple," the embodied "cult"—embraces all of us who are members of the body of Christ. Not only are we an intimate part of Jesus' consecration prayer (John 17), but in all our dimensions, and especially in our bodies, we are also consecrated in and through Christ's sacrificial body. "It is by the will of God that we have been consecrated, through the offering of the body of Jesus Christ once and for all" (Hebrews 10:10).

The human body is not just united with a soul; the person is spirited, being the very expression and evidence of the spiritual dimension. The wounded, alienated person suffers all kinds of breaks and divisions. The redeemed person is intact, having gained an integral wholeness. The devotion to the Sacred Heart should be seen in this perspective. Cardinal Joseph Ratzinger, prefect of the Congregation for the Doctrine of the Faith, indicates this: "The theology of the body proposed by the encyclical *Haurietis Aquas* is an apologia of the heart, of the senses and sentiments."

In Jesus the integrated wholeness of body, soul, and

spirit has become love "made flesh." It is not enough to say that God has revealed his love through the Body of Christ; his body itself is revelation of God's love.

For some time, the devotion to the Sacred Heart was burdened by the needless proposition that the physical heart of Jesus is the seat of all his love. This proposition was one of the main reasons the Holy See was reluctant to approve any liturgical proposal that might be somehow marked by it. In his treatise *Novena to the Sacred Heart*, St. Alphonsus rejected the proposition and thus helped remove obstacles. Already at that time, he insisted that the human brain was the seat of affective life. Yet, the heart remains the basic symbol of embodied love, and in it all movements of affection and sentiment are really felt.

All parts of Holy Scripture, Old and New Testaments alike, make frequent use of this symbol, thereby attesting to the biblical emphasis on bodily, visible, tangible realities. The word "heart" appears even in the pivotal beatitude: "How blest are those whose hearts are pure; they shall see God" (Matthew 5:8).

The truth that our body is a temple of God provides us with an essential motive for a holy life, especially for watchfulness over intentions, affections, and conduct. "Surely, you know that you are God's temple, where the Spirit of God dwells. Anyone who destroys God's temple will himself be destroyed by God, because the temple of God is holy, and that temple you are" (1 Corinthians 3:16–17). "Do you not know that your bodies are limbs and organs of Christ?" (1 Corinthians 6:15).

This notion of the body applies not only to a Christian view of chastity (See 1 Corinthians 6:19) but also to all our moral and religious life. Prime consideration must be given to the ordering of our affective lives, which tangibly involves our hearts but is also an important determining factor in all our desires, decisions, and conduct.

As Christians, then, we cannot separate our beings into spheres and parts, bodies and souls. And in the spontaneous devotion to the Sacred Heart, when we speak of the love of Jesus, we cannot abstract it from his bodily heart. The heart is always the symbol of the center of one's being and thus of wholeness and integration. The whole person is to become embodied love.

Prayer

Most loving Savior, from your first to last breath and heartbeat, you considered and honored your body as a gift of the Father. All your bodily life, and especially your sensitive heart, praised the Father. Your battered body was the most admirable prayer of total abandonment into the hands of the Father, a prayer for us.

Now we look up to your glorified body, yearning to find our beatitude in its splendor and to contemplate it in all eternity. We see your heart as the fountain of love for heaven and earth. Heaven has no need for a splendid temple; your body is the beauty that delights all saints. Your heart is the Holiest of Holies in this eternal temple.

The loving heart of your glorified body draws us to you. There, we have the firmest promise of eternal life. Help us, by the power of your Spirit, to honor our own and our neighbors' bodies as temples of the Holy Spirit, to be invested totally in the service of adoring and serving love.

With great trust, we look to your heart and ask you to enlighten and strengthen us with your grace. Grant us the wisdom to use all the noble faculties of our souls and all the energies of our bodies in your service and for the benefit of the redeemed.

Amen.

29

HEART OF JESUS, VICTOR OVER GODLESSNESS

Knowing God, they have refused to honor him as God, or to render him thanks. Hence, all their thinking has ended in futility, and their misguided minds are plunged in darkness. They boast of their wisdom, but they have made fools of themselves.... Thus, because they have not seen fit to acknowledge God, he has given them up to their own depraved reason. This leads them to break all rules of conduct. They are filled with every kind of injustice, mischief, rapacity, and malice; they are one mass of envy, murder, rivalry, treachery, and malevolence; whisperers and scandal-mongers, hateful to God, insolent, arrogant, and boastful...they show no loyalty to parents, no conscience, no fidelity to their plighted word; they are without natural affection and without pity.

ROMANS 1:21–22,28–31

HEART OF JESUS, VICTOR OVER GODLESSNESS

The devotion to the Sacred Heart had a time of great flowering before and during the French Revolution (1789–1799) when influential segments of society in France and the neighboring countries turned away from faith in Christ. The veneration was understood as a call for merciful love in the face of harmful desertions. Today's situation is even more dramatic. Godlessness spreads in many forms.

On the existential level, we become godless when we sever ourselves from the love of God. We radicalize this alienation when we also theoretically deny the God who is Love. A society whose members are "heartless and without pity" has become godless even before the existence of God is denied.

The most implicit and monstrous godlessness is socialized Marxian atheism, which interprets history as a relentless class war that leads to a classless society. This interpretation opposes Christian faith in God, who has created us all out of love and for love. Surely, this is a godlessness that is "heartless and without pity."

Contained within this aggressive form of atheism and practiced by others even not of the party, there are many gods that separate the human person from God: self-glorification, which leads to explicit refusal to adore a personal God; arrogance; lust for power; terrorism; senseless arms races; and merciless consumerism that inflict cruel injustices on the rest of humanity.

Add to this shocking picture the hidden atheism in the hearts and conduct of many people who call themselves Christians, while their thinking and lifestyle are contaminated and largely directed by practical and theoretical atheism.

Only a living faith in the God of Love, who has revealed himself in Jesus, can destroy these false gods and unmask the various forms of godlessness. Only if our inmost being is filled with the message of love and its transforming grace, and if we turn wholeheartedly to this love, which is symbolized in the heart of Jesus, can we guard our hearts and build in the world around us effective dams against this threatening flood of godlessness.

In the present world situation, Christian faith calls more than ever for firm resolution, a radical option for the reign of love. We become credible witnesses insofar as this option takes hold of our whole being, our thoughts, desires, affections, memories, and wills.

In his solemn prayer in which he reveals his inmost heart, Jesus shows us the way to oppose godlessness in the world: "May they all be one: as thou, Father, art in me, and I in thee, so also may they be in us, that the world may believe that thou didst send me" (John 17:21).

Jesus made known to his disciples the tender and strong love for which the Father sent him into the world. It is also in view of this mission, which he entrusts to us, that he wants to draw us to his heart and fill us with his love, so that we can bring it into the world. Jesus sends us out with and for the same love that he has revealed: "I made thy name known to them, and will make it known, so that the love thou hadst for me may be in them, and I may be in them" (John 17:26).

We can briefly define the scope of the devotion to the Sacred Heart in this way: it is learning to love Jesus and to love with Jesus. This is what the world, threatened by lovelessness and godlessness, needs most urgently. Only a heart glowing with Christ-like love can effectively repel all forms of hidden and open atheism. Only such a love can unmask all disguises of unbelief, and only the greatest love can find the remedies that humankind needs so desperately in this era of unbelief and godlessness.

At this crucial decision-making time in history, all who are captured by the heartfelt love of Christ must join hands and hearts for a common witness to faith bearing fruit in love and justice.

Prayer

O heart full of love, O kindly light and fiery flame, you have come to heal the wounded world; for this, you "set fire to the earth," desiring that it be kindled. (See Luke 12:49.) But, for this confused world, you are also the sign that forces each of us to make our own choice. The outcome that you desire and that you make possible by grace is the reign of peace and salvation, a result of faithful love in harmony with the honor of the heavenly Father. Those who reject your love doom themselves to the reign of darkness, deception, hatred, and enmity.

Lord, I want to decide firmly and forever to love you with all my heart, and I am ashamed that, in the past, I have offended you often by inconsistency and halfheartedness. Looking at your loving heart, I begin to realize the magnitude of this injustice. If I love with only half my heart, I have not yet really acknowledged you as my God. I also see it as a terrible injustice to humankind, which is so much in need of people who show by their lives what it is to adore God as God.

O faithful heart of Jesus, change us, enlighten us, and strengthen us in this time of disunity. Help us Christians join together in strong faith and faithful love, so that the world may believe and find the truth of life. We know that an infinitely merciful God is concerned with fatherly love for all his creatures. O Lord, free the godless from their misery and emptiness.

Beloved Savior, it is frightening to observe that so many Christians are apathetic and slothful. Awaken us all, fill us with new zeal and enthusiasm, and show us the most effective ways to proclaim our faith in you and in the heavenly Father.

Amen.

30

HEART OF JESUS, SOURCE OF PEACE IN OUR WORLD

Let Christ's peace be arbiter in your hearts; to this peace you were called as members of a single body. And be filled with gratitude. Let the message of Christ dwell among you in all its richness.

COLOSSIANS 3:15–16

HEART OF JESUS, SOURCE OF PEACE IN OUR WORLD

In his encyclical *Haurietis Aquas,* Pope Pius XII gave the devotion to the Sacred Heart a program of peace: "Let all who proudly call themselves Christians be fully committed to the kingdom of God on earth. Let them choose the devotion to the Heart of Jesus as a distinctive sign and source of unity, salvation, and peace."

Configuration of the hearts of believers to the heart of Jesus is made known by the fruits of the Spirit: "The harvest of the Spirit is love, joy, peace, patience, kindness, goodness, fidelity, gentleness, and self-control" (Galatians 5:22–23). "Love, joy, and peace" form the core, or heart, of this rich harvest. All the other distinctive qualities of the redeemed are signs of a peaceful heart and serve as the "armor" of peacemakers.

The first inalienable condition for our peace mission is to make Christ's peace the "arbiter in our hearts." But the Letter to the Colossians also makes clear that Christ's disciples see peace as a calling that concerns all members of a single body. We may think of the Church as first and foremost "the body of Christ," but we may also think of it as the whole of humankind for whom Christ died and is risen. As Christians, if we are grateful for the gift of peace, and if the gospel of peace dwells in our hearts in all its richness, we will be committed to peace for everyone on earth.

Christ in person is our reconciliation and peace. In him, the saving plan of God, the design for peace, is revealed and fulfilled. By consecration to the heart of Jesus and by participating in the consecration of the world to his heart, we experience in our inmost being what God tells us through the prophet Jeremiah, who writes that the Lord's plans for the Israelites are plans of peace and prosperity, not misfortune and disaster (see Jeremiah 29:11).

But we must not forget the condition clearly spelled out in the words: "When you seek me, you shall find me; if you seek me with all your heart, I will let you find me" (Jeremiah 29:13). We can call for peace and serve the cause of peace among all people only when our hearts are turned wholly to God. This is precisely the aim of devotion to the Sacred Heart. Turning to the heart of Jesus with a grateful heart means encountering the Redeemer of the world.

Whoever tastes the peace flowing from Jesus' heart will also learn that this very peace—the undeserved gift of the Redeemer—wants to be the arbiter in our hearts, telling us how we are to fulfill our calling to peace "as members of a single body."

The first response of a grateful heart to the gift of peace with God and personal peace of heart will be a strong desire that all may rejoice in this same peace. Christ's faithful disciples will radiate peace, fulfilling the prophecy: "Streams of living water shall flow out from within him" (John 7:38). The peace mission, in the first place, is a kind of "overflow of the peace-filled heart." But this alone does not suffice.

Each of us, according to our charism, capacity, and state in life, is meant to work as a peacemaker with all our competence and persistence. Motivated by gratitude to do this, our hearts will be widened to receive an even greater portion of the Messianic peace. The most serious peace researchers of our time have realized that commitment to peace is a long-term task and that the most decisive part is the formation of peace-loving and peacemaking people and groups.

A theology of the heart of the human person, and especially of the heart of Jesus, reaches the same conclusion but with even greater evidence and emphasis. Our first and most urgent contribution to the peace of the world is the configuration of our hearts with the heart of the Prince of Peace and his "thoughts of peace."

Those who believe in the beatitudes as saving rules in God's kingdom are drawn powerfully to the heart of Jesus when they understand his promise: "How blest are the peacemakers; God shall call them his sons" (Matthew 5:9). By being wholly one with Christ and totally dedicated to his mission as Reconciliator, we are sons and daughters with the only Son of God.

The blessing of the peacemakers is preceded by the beatitude that reads, "How blest are those whose hearts are pure; they shall see God" (Matthew 5:8). Human hearts can be truly "pure" only when thoroughly filled with the all-embracing love of Jesus, for we are simply and thoroughly created and redeemed for that love. If we give love all the space in our hearts and our wills, there will be no space for any impure kind of love or desire.

The peace of Christ, which leaps for joy in our hearts and is our only arbiter, exerts marvelous powers to build personal bridges from heart to heart as well as in and between human communities. This peace is given to all who "draw water with joy from the springs of salvation." Thus, gradually, through mutual help, we discover in ourselves and in others the inner resources that come from God. This renewed faith in the good in ourselves and others is indispensable for our peace mission.

As a result of this, there develops the eminent art of nonviolent commitment to peace and to peaceful solutions of conflicts. This trust in our inner resources is recommended by St. Paul: "My friends, I have no doubt in my own mind that you yourselves are quite full of goodness and equipped with knowledge of every kind, well able to give advice to one another; nevertheless, I have written to refresh your memory" (Romans 15:14–15).

But Paul also points to the art of mobilizing these resources: "Never pay back evil for evil. Let your aims be such as all men count honorable. If possible, so far as it lies with you, live at peace with all men. If your enemy is hungry, feed him; if he is thirsty, give him a drink; by doing this, you will heap live coals on his head. Do not let evil conquer you, but use good to defeat evil" (Romans 12:17–21).

The image of "heaping live coals on the head" needs explanation. It is taken from the experience of the housewife of ancient times, who, after cooking, gathered the live coals at the head of the hearth so that the fire in the house would never fail. Thus, in our relations with our neighbors, especially with someone who causes trouble, we discover and gather all our inner resources of goodness and let the other feel that, despite all difficulties, we believe that he or she, too, has resources for goodness and truth. This means "to speak truth in love" and thus serve the cause of peace in justice and justice in peace.

The purpose of nonviolent action in the face of conflict is not to destroy our adversary. On the contrary, it is based on the trust that the other person can become a friend, a friend of truth, justice, and peace. If our heart is firmly set on this course, we can hope that the other will eventually respond to this appeal, this offer of trust. Such trust is authentic and efficacious if it is grounded in God.

The art of creative nonviolence must be learned and exercised in shared endeavors. But it is most important that the inner resources of the peace-missioner be constantly assured by "drawing water with joy from the springs of salvation"—from Christ, the Prince of Peace, through the power of his Spirit.

In this way, many people may first follow the road that leads to Christ before they come to explicit faith in Christ. This happens because of their experiences with peace-radiating and peacemaking believers who reveal by their conduct the fountain of these inner resources, the "springs of salvation."

We need to understand that, in the long run, not even a minimum of world peace can be guaranteed by endless armament races and mutual threats of annihilation. The longer this inhumane situation continues, the greater becomes the risk that what nobody wants to happen will happen. Meanwhile, the mutual dialogue between nations continues to rapidly deteriorate. Just to speak of deterrence is already the beginning of the destruction of one's own humanity and of the conditions for true reconciliation.

Decades ago, we frequently heard of "moral armament," and, thanks be to God, many gave it high priority over military armament. But what we need here and now is a firm peace covenant, the preparation of which should have top priority. And that requires more than mere "moral re-armament."

Paul's Letter to the Ephesians tells us what we need: "Find your strength in the Lord, in his mighty power. Put on all the armor that God provides.…Take up God's armor; then you will be able to stand your ground when things are at their worst, to complete every task and still to stand. Let the shoes on your feet be the gospel of peace, to give you firm footing; and, with all these, take up the great shield of faith, with which you will be able to quench all the flaming arrows of the Evil One. Take salvation for helmet; for sword, take that which the Spirit gives you—the words that come from God" (Ephesians 6:10–17).

In this perspective and with this spirit of the gospel of peace, nations should train in "re-armament" for energetic and just nonviolence, for peaceful conflict solutions, and for mutual respect and trust. We must learn this and pray for this on all levels, beginning with family life. Christians should be leaders in this approach, inspired by faith in the gospel of peace.

It is true that "armament" with and for a nonviolent commitment to justice and peace will also unmask injustice, hypocrisy, and all forms of violence, but if these actions are done in accord with the eminent art of truth in love, in shared search for a thoroughly humane peace, they will succeed.

Whoever does not see that such a program is most fitting for those who venerate the Sacred Heart has not yet understood anything I have written here.

Prayer

We praise you, Father, Lord of heaven and earth, for having sent us your beloved Son, Jesus Christ, to be our reconciliation and our peace. We cherish your "thoughts of peace," which you have revealed in Jesus.

We firmly believe that you intend to give us the fullness of your peace, because you have sent the One who, in person, is our Peace. We thank you for the wisdom of peace in our hearts and for our vocation to be peacemakers, thus proving that we truly are your children. We thank you also for having given us, in our age, men and women who radiate peace and are wholly dedicated to the cause of peace and reconciliation.

Merciful Father, in Jesus' name we implore you to forgive us our many sins against peace and our negligence in fostering it. Grant us, as a sign of your forgiveness, a burning zeal and constant faithfulness in promoting the causes of peace in our hearts, in our families and communities, in our Church, and in the entire world. Let there be peace among nations in justice and mutual respect.

O heart of our Redeemer, fountain of salvation and love, you have consecrated yourself totally to peace, to the glory of your Father, and for our salvation. Together with you, we want to consecrate ourselves anew to the cause of peace. For when you consecrated yourself before your death, you took us, your disciples, into that all-embracing consecration. Lord, accept our renewed consecration and grant us your Spirit so that we may be consecrated in truth. May all our life bear fruit in love, joy, and peace.

Amen.

About the Author

Rev. Bernard Häring, CSsR (1912–1998), was a Redemptorist—a writer, scholar, pastor, and preacher. More importantly, this renowned theologian is remembered as a kind, humble, and prayerful man.

www.ingramcontent.com/pod-product-compliance
Lightning Source LLC
Chambersburg PA
CBHW032037150426
43194CB00006B/318